Scottish school leavers write
about school and life afterwards

TELL THEM
FROM ME

Edited and introduced by
LESLEY GOW and
ANDREW McPHERSON

ABERDEEN UNIVERSITY PRESS

First published 1980
Aberdeen University Press
A member of the Pergamon Group

© Centre for Educational Sociology
University of Edinburgh 1980

British Library Cataloguing in Publication Data
Tell them from me
1. High school students—Scotland
2. High school graduates—Scotland
3. Unemployment—Scotland
I. Gow, Lesley   II. McPherson, Andrew
373.1'8'0922   LA656.7

ISBN 08-025738-0
ISBN 08-025739-9 Pbk

PRINTED IN GREAT BRITAIN
THE UNIVERSITY PRESS
ABERDEEN

'PLEASE READ THIS
DON'T IGNORE IT
THAT'S WHAT YOU
PROBABLY WOULD
HAVE DONE. . .'

School leaver

Contents

Acknowledgements

This book uses material from research supported in the Centre for Educational Sociology at the University of Edinburgh by the Social Science Research Council (HR 3262), the Scottish Education Department and the Manpower Services Commission. An additional small grant from the Scottish Education Department greatly helped with the preparation of this volume. We are grateful to all these bodies. Edith Cope was the first to appreciate the full value of the school leavers' writings in the 1977 survey and John Gray was the first to suggest that a selection might be published. Thanks are due to both these former members of the CES for their insight and for their work on the material. We must also thank Osnat Harari and Hugh Kernohan for assisting with the analysis of the leavers' accounts in the 1977 survey, and Adam Redpath and Joanne Lamb for help with computing. Margaret MacDougall and Vivien Thain ably prepared the manuscript and, with Mary Kerr, typed many more accounts than those finally used here. Willi Bremner allowed one of us to discuss a selection of these writings with pupils at Wester Hailes Education Centre. Colleagues in the Centre for Educational Sociology were generous with their advice. Other than in the leavers' writings, we alone are responsible for the views expressed or for any errors there may be. Finally, we are grateful to all the respondents to the CES surveys of school leavers whether or not they added their own account and whether or not it is to be found in our selection.

CHAPTER ONE

WHAT SORT OF BOOK IS THIS?

What sort of book is this? What is it about?

The accounts that follow have been written by young people who left school in Scotland in the second half of the 1970s. Some of them tell us about their experiences at school and about what it was like to take examinations and then start a job or a course in college or university. Others, however, write about a somewhat different set of experiences. They tell us what it was like to truant from school, or to be in a class that was offered only a meagre curriculum and no prospect of sitting public examinations. They also write about leaving school to find that there were no jobs to be had, or no jobs that they wanted.

Altogether these accounts tell us what has been happening to pupils at school and in the months after they have left. The book is about their experience, their opinions and feelings, about their grudges and their gratitude. It is about the way education, work and unemployment seemed to young people—and especially to the less fortunate among them—as the seventies drew to a close.

For reasons that will be explained, the selection of writings gives particular prominence to the experience of pupils and leavers who achieved few academic qualifications whilst at school, if any at all. In recent years, roughly 30 per cent of Scottish secondary pupils could be described as 'non-certificate' in that their third and fourth year courses did not lead to their sitting the Scottish Certificate of Education (SCE). A further fifteen per cent or so of pupils have been presented by their schools for the SCE O grade examination, but they have failed to attain any awards in the range A, B, C. Before the 'banding' arrangement of 1973 which removed the pass/fail distinction from O grade awards, attainments below the C grade would have been regarded as failures. Almost half of Scottish pupils, then, approach the end of their school life with little or no hope of attaining a substantial qualification. What have their last years at school been like; what are their prospects at a time of increasing competition for jobs, and how do they feel about their schooling once it is over?

The reactions of non-certificate pupils and leavers are of particular importance. Many of them reject school and feel rejected by it; they truant more often, are disciplined more often and face unemployment more often than other pupils and leavers. They are also more likely to have problems with the basic skills of reading, writing and computation. These considerations alone make it important to understand the viewpoint of those to whom school appears to offer very little. They may also, incidentally, explain why it is that the writing of the non-certificate leavers often has particular qualities of feeling and insight, qualities of the person whom circumstances have made sceptical, detached and sometimes cynical or angry. Perhaps such reactions allow us to disregard the writers' views; or perhaps we should listen especially hard to outsiders.

The writings assembled here can be read and judged in several different ways. First and foremost they are about individual lives; a collection of autobiographical sketches, a little under four hundred in all. Many are brief and unrealised, reflecting sometimes unwittingly the quality of the school years themselves. Often however, the writing is vigorous and direct, the product of the authors' all-too-clear views as to what they had made of the little that they thought was on offer.

These qualities give this collection a second character, that of an anthology, sometimes of the best writing of young people about school and after, and sometimes of the writing that is the most revealing: 'I was never at school but I am always at my work I am never off I hate being off my work it is so interesting but school is boring.' The girl who wrote this described her work as 'under-presser.

3

Press the tip's and seam's of ties'. And the advantage of work over school? 'At work you can talk and have a laugh and still do your own number but at school you talk and get the belt'. How much more would school have had to do in order to do better than this?

In such cases the arresting quality, not so much of the writing but of the instances, and of what is left unsaid or taken for granted, suggests a third way in which we might react. We can also read these accounts and stories as news, as a set of despatches, not always from the front, but often from areas that many of us have not seen at first hand. Tell them from me. Tell whom? Well, first perhaps, the generations who have left school in times of full employment. 'School. Forgotten Children. I was a girl that was not very good at my work. We were all put into a group and forgoten. there was no hope for us. but there is we can all work. My two little sisters are the same. (forgotten children) Help them please. They need help I hope they do something for them.' The young woman who wrote this had left school without certification and had been unemployed for over a year. Her story bears the marks of two developments whose concurrence has created for the young new areas of experience that many of today's parents have not known. It took almost thirty years for our society to realise its commitment to the extension of compulsory schooling to sixteen years and it is taking even longer to develop forms of education that are appropriate to the needs, interests and abilities of many children who are now kept at school until they are sixteen. But by the time the first year-groups of such children, the ROSLA children (ROSLA-raising of the school leaving age), were coming out of school in the years after 1973, we were also seeing a dramatic rise in the levels of unemployment among young people, unemployment that may be a feature of the economies of most advanced industrial societies for years to come. The unemployment rate amongst non-certificate leavers in Scotland has been much higher than that among leavers who had examination qualifications. New routes are emerging to new areas of experience, and this book tells us about some of them.

Tell them from me. 'Them' include the helping agencies that pupils think should exist to cope with this new situation: '(Forgoten children). Help them please. they need help I hope they do something for them.' Again, 'them' are the people whom the leavers think are indirectly responsible: 'Why do all the onces at 20-40 get a job so easily? As I have been interviewed by millions of people and not yet got a job. We school leavers all have to get started somewhere just like other people.' And 'them' are the pupils who are coming through the schools today: '. . if only the teacher could convince the pupils that the last 2 years at schools are really important. I think that almost everyone who leaves school with no grades at all regret that they didn't try hard enough and allways wish they had another chance'.

And 'them', of course, are also the people whom the leavers see as most directly involved, the teachers with whom they have lived much of the last four years of their lives: 'The reason I never went to school the last year was because I was in a non sertificate class and the teachers had no time for dunces. we did not get any work of any kind everyday at our different classes we just sat all day doing nothing and our exams last year were adding sums "at our age". It was terrible that was the only reason 4th year of 4D and 4C never went to school because I liked going to school up (to) then. Well that's all I have to say. I would like to have said that to some of the teachers at _____ Academy'; or again, '. . But now I feel sorry for the people in school the only thing in my point of view to help pupils now is the teachers listen to the children's views and realise how STRONG the pupils feel . . .'

The voices that follow, then, are those of pupils and young school leavers, often outraged, sometimes stunned and sometimes close to despair. Some are opinionated and others just plain unperceptive; sometimes this may go with academic failure at school, but it may also accompany success. Certainly the successes of the educational system, if that is what we may call the bare majority of pupils who leave school with their clutch of certificates, have no monopoly of insight into the complexities of life for pupils and teachers. The leaver whom we have just read urging teachers to heed the strength of pupils' feelings had herself resisted the school's efforts to persuade her to 'study her subjects' rather than continue with the part-time job she had started when a fourteen year old pupil. She tells her full story later on, ending like this: '. . . it could have had me on the DOLE as well if I had listened. By saying this I dont mean the pupil to be just stubern but to listen and think very carefully before commitment. But this all lies inbetween both the pupils' and teachers ALSO PARENTS to help and understand I also realise that the teachers have a ruff time to look after the pupils and teache them I also wish the teachers the best of luck they need it. As I think this is a very good idea to give pupils this form I also hope this help's pupils and also teachers as teachers need as much help as pupils and the teachers have a lot to contend with.'

Why give pupils and school leavers a voice? It is intended as no disrespect to the young adults whose writings make up this book to mention something that W. J. Weatherby recently wrote in the *Guardian*: 'What we lack for a real understanding is the voice of children talking to themselves or to each other on the deepest, most truthful level, and adults are never allowed to eavesdrop on that. One imagines some kind of secret testimony, like one of the samizdat documents passed around in the Soviet underground, which very young children might circulate among themselves, adding their own statements before handing it on. Like the Soviet secret police, adults would have to steal a copy to sneak a look into these children's minds—children to whom even teenagers are untrustworthy, because teenagers are already half-adults' (16.11.79).

In fact there has been a growing interest in recent years in the writings of children or of 'half-adults', an interest that testifies perhaps to two concerns: to a concern among adults to understand better young persons' hopes and fears about the social world that awaits them; and, second, to the attempts of the young to fashion their *own* consciousness of their *own* world and to shape it for themselves. Edward Blishen's *The School That I'd Like* is an example of the first concern; and *Letter to a Teacher* by the School of Barbiana is a product of the second. We recognise increasingly that there is a voice to be heard, a voice that usually speaks, of course, through less conventional means than the pages contained between the covers of a book like this.

Why then give the voice this platform? Are the things that school leavers say truthful and honest; are they fair; are they insightful? Above all, many will ask, are they representative and is the selection presented here a representative selection? Some readers may wish to turn these questions over in their minds when trying to form a reaction to the accounts that follow. They are relevant questions and we shall try to answer them on their merits. But before this one might perhaps reflect on two further questions. First, to what extent does one feel that the status of the writing of children and teenagers is questionable precisely because they are regarded as 'half-adults', or something less? Is this a reasonable attitude? And, second is the issue of representativeness to be decisive in persuading one to take seriously a young person's account of what has happened to him or her? When we read a conventional biography, or when we simply take an interest in another person's life, the question of whether that life is 'representative' of something else is not very central to our response. It is precisely because a person's life is what it is that it claims our recognition; and this claim does not diminish because it is one of many. If anything, what is then diminished is our own capacity to recognise and respond to the many individualities. Our view of the world shapes and is shaped in many ways by the relatively few people we meet and know. Only in very special circumstances do we ask if our experience of the world is representative. The writings in this book enlarge our experience of the world and their authority is the authority of experience. A girl who had a long story to tell about how she felt her school had unfairly stopped her 'working her way up a class' finished it like this: 'I'm quite intelligent really but you just don't get a chance to show what you can do teachers just don't help at all. It isn't a grudge against anybody it's just I know it happened to me.' And if we know things when they happen to us, then so do 'half-adults' when they happen to them. Nevertheless, there remain problems with how we evaluate such knowledge, with how we set it against competing claims and with how we represent it to others.

Whose writings are these and why did they write?
We may read what follows, then, as biography, anthology, news or simply as messages directed to us by those who see us as 'them'. But still the question remains, in what ways can we also read these writings as evidence and as evidence in what sense? Who wrote these accounts; what questions were they answering; whom did they think they were addressing and why?

The material comes from two very similar postal surveys of representative samples of Scottish school leavers conducted in 1977 and 1979, generally about nine months after their leaving school. All stages of the surveys were conducted according to the usual rules and procedures of survey research, and response rates of around 80 per cent were achieved from leavers at all levels, whether they left school with no qualifications whatsoever or with enough examination passes to take them straight into higher education. The sampling fractions were 40 per cent in 1977 and either 10 or 20 per cent, depending on level of qualification, in 1979.[1] The questions were mainly of the 'fixed-alternative' type that required the respondent to answer by choosing from among the categories provided. Statistical analysis and publication of this material has been continuous since 1977 and has provided a backdrop against which decisions have been taken about the selection and presentation of the writings in this book. The accounts written by the school leavers themselves were volunteered in response to an invitation to respondents to add further comments on the blank back page of the questionnaire. Thus the quantitative information from the statistical analyses of the fixed-alternative questions and the qualitative, open-ended writings of the respondents provide us with two, linked perspectives on the opinions and experiences of recent school leavers.

The topics covered in the surveys varied somewhat according to the examination level of the leaver. Table 1 in the Appendix shows the percentages of leavers who attained different levels of presentation and award in the mid seventies. The official figures for the whole population of school leavers are shown and these are

[1] Fuller details of the 1977 survey may be found in Raffe, Lamb *et al.* (1978).

compared with the figures from the 1977 sample survey which are given in a little more detail. The 1977 survey in fact aimed to sample only about three quarters of the leaving population—certain regions were excluded—whereas the 1979 survey covered all regions. However, differences between the percentages in Table 1, based on the official population figures, and those based on the 1977 sample survey are trivial. The figures show that about one third of the school population (35 per cent) left school without achieving a recognised award in the Scottish Certificate of Education (SCE) examinations and that just under one third (31 per cent) never sat an SCE examination. Opinions vary, and feelings are often aroused, over the various terms that may be used to describe such pupils—'unqualified' attracts particular hostility—but pupils who sat no SCE examinations we here call 'non-certificate' (and sometimes 'non-SCE'). In using this term no account is taken of either local certificates or of English CSE certificates that may have been attempted. The percentage of Scottish leavers sitting English examinations is small, though growing in the case of the Certificate of Secondary Education. No slight is intended by the use of the term 'non-certificate'. Equally, no approbation is intended by our use of the term 'O grade leavers' for those who attempted SCE O (but not H) grades (40 per cent of leavers); or of the terms 'H grade leavers' and 'Highers' leavers' for those who attempted the Higher grade of the SCE (30 per cent of leavers). In saying this we recognise that the common equation of personal worth with academic attainment may, for many readers, invest these terms with more meanings than we intend, meanings that will become perfectly plain in the pages of leavers' writings that follow.

The topics covered in the surveys varied somewhat according to the examination level, if any, of the leaver: Highers leavers answered a 16 page questionnaire, O grade leavers a 12 page questionnaire and non-certificate leavers one of only 6 pages. These different 'levels' of questionnaire themselves came in different versions that were administered to random sub-sets of the sample. All versions of all the levels of questionnaire, however, asked certain questions in common. These included the leavers' evaluations of their schooling; the help they felt they had received from careers officers and others; the subjects studied and examinations taken, where relevant and the record of their transition to further education or training, or to work or unemployment. All leavers were also asked whether they had truanted in their fourth year at school and many were asked whether they had received corporal punishment. On the back of all questionnaires in the 1977 and 1979 surveys was the statement: 'The National School Leavers Survey aims to provide information on the views and experiences of school leavers to help improve education and related services. It is run independently by the Centre for Educational Sociology at Edinburgh University.'

The framing of the invitation to write more on the back page varied in several ways, mostly minor, between the 1977 and 1979 surveys, and between the different 'levels' of questionnaire. The 1977 questionnaires for Highers and O grade leavers simply asked 'Have you any comments?'.

Those for the leavers who had not attempted any SCE exams asked: 'Would you like to tell us a little bit more about yourself? We would like to hear what you have to say. What did you like about your last year at school? What didn't you like? How could your teachers have made the time more useful? What have you done since you left school? Tell us about your job and about looking for one. Please write on this page. But don't worry about spelling.'

Approximately 30 per cent of the accounts in this book come from the 1977 survey, the remainder coming from that of 1979. The invitation to non-certificate leavers in 1979 was modified slightly as follows: 'Would you like to tell us a little bit more about yourself? We would like to hear what you have to say. What did you like about your school? What didn't you like? What have you found difficult at work or when looking for work? What should be done to help young people who are looking for jobs? Please write on this page. But don't worry about spelling.' And in 1979 fuller prompts were given to the O grade and H grade leavers. These were, respectively: (for O grade leavers) 'We hope this questionnaire has let you say what you feel about school. If there is anything else you would like to say, this page is for you to tell us in your own words. For instance, is what you learned at school useful to you now? What was good about your school? What could be made better? What advice would you give to someone still at school?'' (and for Highers leavers) 'We hope this questionnaire has given you a chance to express your own views about school and the process of leaving it. If there are other things which you think are important, this page is for you to describe them in your own words. For instance, has what you learned at school proved relevant to what you are doing now? What aspects of your schooling were good? What aspects do you think could be improved? What advice would you give to a secondary pupil in the light of your own experience?'

Which respondents tended to write extended comments? One's first guess might be: those who were accustomed to using the written word as a medium of communication; that is, the more able school leavers. And one's second guess might be: those who had something to complain about, who had a chip on their shoulder or felt they had something to blame school for. Surprisingly both intuitions are wide of the mark.

The following extract from Table 8 in the Appendix shows the percentages who commented among all who replied to the questionnaire. Separate figures are given for the two surveys (1977 and 1979), for the three questionnaire levels, and for boys and girls. In 1977 it was the non-certificate respondents who commented most often, and especially the girls among them (63 per cent of whom volunteered comments). In 1979, when the invitation to H and O grade leavers was elaborated, the respondents at these two levels commented more often than their counterparts had in 1977 but O grade boys and girls were still less likely to comment in 1979 than were non-certificate respondents. Almost half the non-certificate boys and about half the Highers boys wrote something. But the proportion was again highest among girl respondents in the non-certificate group. Two thirds of them had something extra to say.

Percentages of respondents that volunteered comments

	1977			1979	
	boys	girls		boys	girls
Highers respondents	36	35		49	50
O grade respondents	25	29		36	49
non-SCE respondents	46	63		51	67

(extract from Appendix, Table 8)

Was it the dissatisfied, the unfortunate and the moaners who tended to respond to the invitation to tell their story on the back page of the questionnaire? We may judge this by looking at the percentages that volunteered comments, making

further distinctions among them according to their answers to a small selection of
the relevant fixed-alternative items in the two surveys. The finer detail is given,
again, in Table 8 in the Appendix. The percentages are shown according to
whether or not respondents had thought their last year at school was 'worthwhile'
and whether or not they had 'enjoyed' it; according to the degree to which they
said they had played truant and the frequency with which they said they had been
physically punished; and, finally, according to whether, when they answered the
questionnaire, they were in full-time employment or full-time education, or were
unemployed. These items were used because they relate to the main themes in
terms of which the selection of comments has been arranged. Also, in judging
these comments, we need to know the extent, if any, to which pupils and leavers
who had had 'bad' experiences, as indicated by their answers to the fixed-
alternative items, volunteered their views more often.

In fact the task of selecting the writings for publication was eased considerably
by the fact that respondents accepted the invitation to write about their
experiences at school and after in more or less equal measure, irrespective of
whether or not their experience had been bad. This is particularly true of the non-
certificate respondents who have contributed a large part of the selection that
follows. If we limit ourselves for an example to non-certificate male respondents to
the 1977 survey, we find that among those who said that their last year at school
was worthwhile the percentage that commented was 48 per cent; among those who
said it had not been worthwhile, the percentage that commented was about the
same at 51 per cent. Among non-certificate boys who had enjoyed their last year at
school, 45 per cent commented; among those who said they had not enjoyed their
last year, the percentage was 48; among those who had 'never' been belted in their
last year, or only 'once or twice', 54 and 51 per cent respectively commented;
among the boys who had 'often' been belted, (about a quarter) the percentage that
commented was 51 per cent.

We can safely infer, therefore, that the experience of the non-certificate boys
who wrote about their life at school and thereafter was, in these respects, no more
or less typical than was that of the non-certificate boys who did not write. By
making similar comparisons for girls in the non-certificate group, and for the two
sexes in the 1979 survey we may extend this conclusion (though there was a slight
tendency for girls in the two surveys to comment more often if they had been
physically punished 'quite often' or 'often'). Finally, a comparison of the
unemployed with the employed shows that between six and nine per cent more of
the former added comments, this tendency holding true for the non-certificate
respondents of both sexes in both surveys.

Only in respect of employment, then, were those who commented consistently
a-typical of all non-certificate respondents. Among O grade and Highers
respondents, who are also shown in Table 8, there *was* a tendency for the more
disaffected to write more often about their time at school. The differences were not
large. Nevertheless they appeared fairly consistently for both boys and girls at both
levels of school achievement and in both surveys. What these differences meant, in
practical terms, was that about five or ten per cent more of leavers who had not
'enjoyed' their last year at school, or who had not thought it 'worthwhile', who had
truanted 'several days at a time' or more, or who had been belted 'quite often' or
'often', wrote about their experiences on the back page of the questionnaire. This
means that, were one to form one's impression of the state of the schools solely
from the open-ended writings of the respondents to the questionnaires, one's

conclusions might be slightly biased towards undue pessimism, at least as far as O grade and Highers leavers were concerned.

There is, however, a second set of sampling and response biases that arose earlier during the construction of the samples and the administration of the surveys. Though small, the net effect of these biases acts to bias conclusions towards optimism, *ie* in the *opposite* direction to the effects described above. The detail of this matter is out of all proportion to its relevance to the present argument. Further information is given elsewhere[1] and the bias is mentioned only because it may have done something to counteract any tendency towards undue pessimism that would otherwise occur in conclusions based solely on the open-ended writing of the certificated leavers.

One's overall conclusion is, then, that the open-ended comments were offered by a group of leavers whose experiences closely matched those of all school leavers in Scotland in the later 1970s. Such biases as there were at this stage were probably very small. If anything the accounts paint slightly too optimistic a picture of the experience of non-certificated leavers (except with respect to employment) and slightly too pessimistic a picture of what happened to the certificated leavers. However, the size of such biases as existed was of an order that would give a reader in, say, a hundred scripts, about four or five more 'optimistic' or 'pessimistic' stories, depending on the issue, than there should have been.[2]

Is the writing honest? For whom did leavers think they were writing?

Before explaining in the next section how and why this particular selection of writings was made, it might be helpful to think for a moment about the circumstances in which leavers wrote their accounts. We are not of course eavesdropping on the voice of young people 'talking to themselves or to each other on the deepest, most truthful level'. Nevertheless, there are good reasons to think that the writing was honestly undertaken. The writers were addressing their remarks to a Dr Edith Cope (in 1977) or a Dr Joanne Lamb (in 1979). These two members of the research team had been presented to the respondent as researchers on a survey that aimed 'to provide information on the views and experiences of school leavers to help improve education and related services'. The prompts were either neutral ('Have you any comments?'—Highers and O grade 1977) or invited both positive and negative replies. Those to the Highers and O grade leavers in 1979 also asked 'What advice would you give to a secondary pupil in the light of your own experience?'.

So far as we can judge, many writers, possibly the majority, understood and accepted that they were writing to someone, A 'Doctor', who wanted to know how things were in order to make things better or to pass on advice. What this Doctor already knew about schooling, education, and work could be inferred from the fixed-alternative questions she had asked; and, so far as we can judge, these inferences were generally favourable. Whoever this Doctor was, she obviously knew enough about young persons' experiences to ask questions that were generally sensible and pertinent. Moreover, being a woman, she was possibly seen by many as more approachable than whatever sort of Doctor it was that was implied by a man's name. This is not to say that those who wrote did not include the incredulous, the cynical, the pessimistic and the unforthcoming: 'I am not going to tell you about myself—and I am not intrested in any other people and if

[1] McPherson and Raffe (1978).
[2] This assumes no within-script bias in topic selection; see below.

they had a job or not'; or again, 'Dear Joanne, I don't understand the point of any of this booklet. I think school was a waste of time and so is this booklet. What good could it do for you to know anything about me, or anybody else. I would like to know, to what you have put all of the information you receive I simply couldn't find any use for knowing all about other peoples private lives'; and again, 'Don't ignore this thats what you probably would have done'. However the majority who indicated their view of the researchers' identity and probity appear to have accepted the researchers' explanation: 'I have been so long in returning the questionnaire because I wanted to think very carefully about this page. The six years I spent at secondary school were much appreciated. I am though very critical of the demands made by universities and F.E. colleges for academic qualifications, which influence to a vast extent the curriculum taught in schools. I am also very concerned about education for education's sake . . . .'; and '. . . . That's what I think now its up to you Dr Joanne Lamb.'

Some independent information on whom the respondents thought they were addressing, and why, comes from a small study of 25 leavers who had received the 1977 non-certificate questionnaire. They were interviewed about a fortnight after receipt of the questionnaire by members of the Sociology Department of Moray House College of Education. They found that, of the 25 interviewees, eight thought that the questionnaire had come from 'University', one from a 'woman doctor', one from 'someone interested in schools', two from the careers office and one each from 'students' and 'Moray House'. Four did not know. The remaining seven, however, thought that the school had sent the questionnaire to them. To quote from the conclusions of the Moray House study:

'When we asked respondents what kind of people they thought would be interested in 'this kind of thing', representative replies included "teachers", "higher up people who run the schools", "my housemistress", "careers people" and "people who collect information and find out what's happening"; all fairly realistic answers.

The respondents' perception of the size of the survey is not important in itself, though we got the impression that the survey was seen to be small and local, geared to the needs of their particular school. An impression was formed that many kids, now that they were away from school, relished the prospect of letting their teachers know what they really thought of school. One girl explained that she had spent about an hour completing the questionnaire, and that she had written a story on the back page. She wanted us to emphasise that her "story" was very important.

Most respondents thought that filling in the questionnaire would be very useful, feeling that their experience would "do something to help those leaving school now"; other answers were "It helps other years at school", "It helps others", "It's useful for people in school", "It helps the careers man", "It helps to make schools better". One father interjected: "A really good idea, I wish there was more of it"' (Cosford 1978).

Other views reported by the Moray House study were summarised as a table (overleaf).

There was no immediate audience, other perhaps than parents, brothers and sisters, for what the respondents wrote, no group to play to, no immediate response to be won. Anonymity was explicitly guaranteed. The possibility of publication for their comments was never mentioned. Indeed, at that stage it had not even been envisaged by the research team itself. No doubt the motives for

Opinions about the questionnaire

	Yes	?	No
Was it difficult to fill in?	1	1	20
Did you take it seriously?	17	4	2
Do you think it asked 'sensible' questions?	14	6	3
Do you think this kind of 'research' is useful?	14	4	1
Do you think the answers you gave will let them know exactly how you feel?	14	4	2
Was there any question(s) you found hard to answer?	3	5	10

23 of the 25 interviewees said they had completed and returned the questionnaire. Other missing information for each item results from questions that were not asked or not answered.

writing were more various than the straight forward, cheerful altruism of the person who wrote: 'Tell them not to stop trying because I was out of a job for four months. Tell them from me the sooner they find a job the more people they will meet and be the same way as me happy at my work. I give them my best wishes.'

Questionnaires commonly stimulate the recipients to think about issues and events more deeply, and sometimes from a fresh perspective. Many respondents clearly enjoyed expressing themselves, one revealing that '. . This is the first time I have written anything since I left school.' (The implications of this remark for pupils in transition from school are immense). But, whatever the motives of those who wrote, one's overall impression is that they generally took the job very seriously and wrote honestly about their experiences, feelings and opinions. And perhaps the readers of this book whose use of the written word is effortless should allow that, for many non-certificate respondents, the act of writing, and of writing to a stranger about their own lives, involved a considerable effort in two unfamiliar domains. Some, however, were clearly annoyed at the implication of the questionnaire's advice to them '. . don't worry about spelling.' One boy filled the entire back page with the following, in bold lettering: 'THERE IS NO EMPLOYMENT FOR YOUNG PEOPLE IN _____ IM JOINING THE ARMY. I DIDN'T LIKE SCHOOL AND I CAN SPELL'.[1]

There remains the possibility that, had the accounts been collected in some other way, or at some other time, a different picture might have emerged. Every method of research has disadvantages. One disadvantage of fixed-alternative responses to a postal questionnaire is that an element of uncertainty must remain as to how the question has been construed and as to what is intended by the answer. The open-ended answers tell us more of what respondents meant but even they leave one frustrated on occasion, wishing to probe more, to seek elaboration. But one of the great advantages of the postal questionnaire is precisely that respondents can take time to consider their reply; and in their open-ended writing they may volunteer

---

[1] Several comments on the reliability and honesty of respondents may be added. First, the analyses of data from the school leavers' surveys over a decade have never given cause to doubt the overall honesty of respondents though there will always of course be some sampling and response bias, some failures of memory, and some under-reporting. A particularly relevant check on the reliability of the reports of truancy is described in Cope and Gray (1978). It should be noted that, whilst individual unreliability, in the technical sense, may lead to under-reporting, it only produces bias when it is correlated with germane individual attributes.

accounts that would not be so readily forthcoming to an interviewer in the same room. Moreover, as we have already indicated, the absence of a ready audience for the reply diminishes the likelihood that what will emerge will be tailored to those whom the respondent wishes to impress. We have explained that the postal survey ascribed a somewhat hazy identity to the researcher but gave a fairly explicit statement of the aims of the survey. This form of presentation, and also the content of the questionnaire, will doubtless have influenced the writings of all respondents and we leave it to the reader to judge how far such an influence invalidates the picture that emerged. For our part we believe that the invitation to write was reasonably balanced and that, whilst it may be argued that the general emphasis on 'improvement' and 'help' in our presentation of the survey to leavers may have done something to elicit critical comment among all who commented, it cannot explain away the character and force of the response.

More often than not we have reproduced leavers' entire accounts even though they may sometimes cover a number of the topics that we have tried to organise into separate sections. But the accounts in their entirety often show that leavers who commented critically on some aspects of their schooling had good things to say about other aspects. A whole section of the chapter on corporal punishment and belting, for example, is given over to such passages, and, critical of teachers though many comments were, it was not uncommon for the criticism to be selective. We are unable to reach a definite conclusion on the extent to which, *within any single account*, our presentation of the purposes of the survey has biased the views that we have elicited towards undue criticism or, indeed, in any other direction. But we have two reasons for thinking that the size of any bias towards unduly critical comment is not large. First, as we have said, critical comments were often made selectively with respect to teachers, events and aspects of schooling. Second, we have also been able to show that, on the whole, the leavers who volunteered comments were broadly representative of respondents as a whole. If a serious bias towards undue criticism were occurring within each account as a consequence of the way in which the purpose of the survey was perceived or, to put it another way, if there were certain sorts of 'topic bias' in the accounts, then it is possible that those who commented would, as a group, have been less likely to report in the fixed-alternative questions answered earlier in the questionnaire, that they had, for example, 'enjoyed' their last year at school or found it 'worthwhile'. But this, as we have seen, is not the case.

Nevertheless, although the respondents who volunteered comments were broadly representative of all respondents, we cannot, either logically or empirically, exclude the possibility that, once they had decided to comment, some at least commented mainly on what they had experienced as negative aspects of their schooling. Whether such an orientation constitutes bias can, in part, be left to the reader to judge. The writings that follow may occasionally read as resentful, unperceptive, hostile or partial. But do we feel in reading them that they were offered dishonestly, maliciously or frivolously? Their transparency seems evident and their cumulative impact is convincing. For example the disturbingly similar stories told by leaver after leaver in the opening chapters on belting, truancy and the neglect of non-certificate classes in fact reflect pupils' experiences of more than 80 schools; the events were experienced, and the accounts were written, mainly in isolation one from another. As we shall explain below, no attempt was made in any chapter to select at least one account from each school—the need for brevity would alone have precluded this—but these 80 or so schools nevertheless happen to comprise about a fifth of all Scottish secondary schools. Can we deny the existence of the world that is revealed again and again in the separate stories these leavers tell? And, moving from the individual stories to the more systematic, if more impersonal, picture that emerges from the statistical analyses of the fixed-alternative questionnaire data shown in the tables in the Appendix, do we doubt that what we have is two different perspectives on the same landscape?

Two further considerations that bear on whether and in what ways the respondents' open-ended writings were representative of their views and experience may briefly be mentioned. First, the accounts were collected some nine months after the pupils had left school. Had the accounts been collected earlier or later would they have told the same story about school? Arguably, for example, the more frequent experience of unemployment among non-certificate leavers may have reinforced already negative attitudes towards school. Conversely, success in gaining entry to university may have belatedly convinced a Highers leaver that it had all been worthwhile. What little evidence we have suggests, however, that the immediate post-school experiences of leavers have not greatly influenced their evaluation of their schooling; or, if they have, that leavers can distinguish between earlier and more recent opinions as is illustrated, for example, by the distinction that a number of the writers make between their views at the time of answering the questionnaire and the views that they recall they had held whilst at school: 'The school I was at is one of the toughest in _____ and the teachers are too soft. You found it hard to study when there was a load of evil lads around. . . . But you couldn't ask for a move because if the rest of the class found out you were for it. Nearly every class I went to the teachers were always telling me I was imature and they were damn right. But I wish now they had kept me in line when I think about it. . . .'

More reassuring than such internal evidence is the fact that, once account is taken of the different certification levels of the employed and the unemployed, the latter were no more nor less likely than the former to have judged their last year at school as having been 'worthwhile'. Among unemployed non-certificate leavers in 1975/76, for example, 22 per cent said their last year had been 'worthwhile'; and the percentage was the same among non-certificate leavers in employment. This is not conclusive evidence that any distortion of memory in the light of post-school experience has been small. However, when added to the internal evidence of the accounts themselves, it suggests that, had these accounts been collected as pupils completed their last year, the story they would have told would not have been greatly different. Furthermore, some readers may feel that, in this particular instance, hindsight is a real benefit; that, nine months after leaving school, ex-pupils are in a better position to describe and reflect on their schooling than they would have been earlier.

Consideration of the timing of the surveys of 1977 and 1979 reminds us, secondly, that the leavers of the later seventies had started their secondary education in the immediate aftermath of ROSLA and sometimes in schools or areas that had recently experienced, or were still undergoing, reorganisation along comprehensive lines. In 1971 for example, only about 40 per cent of Scotland's education authority and grant-aided secondary schools were officially designated as all-through six-year comprehensives in that they offered a five- or six-year course to an unselected entry from a catchment area that was fixed for all the six years. Roughly a further 20 per cent of secondary schools offered full courses, but combined a non-selective intake from the immediate catchment area with a selective intake from neighbouring areas. A great variety of schools made up the remaining 40 per cent, but most were selective in that they catered primarily for only one of the two types of pupil that had been recognised under the earlier selective system: the academic or the non-academic. By the mid seventies, however, nearly all of the country's EA secondary schools were either all-through comprehensives or were four-year schools serving isolated communities but offering the possibility of transfer to a neighbouring comprehensive.

To this picture of a secondary system that towards the end of the seventies was beginning to settle after two major changes, we may add any number of further factors that may also have affected the schooling that pupils have received in recent years. The emergence of provision for pupil guidance and of new structures for teacher promotion, high rates of staff turnover and staff shortages in some areas, teacher strikes and workings to rule, part-time education and restrictions on public spending—all of these, along with regionalisation in 1975 may have combined, it could be argued, to give to the education received by pupils in the seventies its own special character. At the time of writing, however, it is difficult to be confident that many of the implications of the seventies for the next decade can easily be discarded. In what senses have the last ten years of our experience been a-typical?

It may be helpful at this point to summarise what has so far been said about the status of the leavers' writings from which the following selection has been made. The size, source and likely nature of some of the biases in the writings are as follows:

i) arising from survey sampling procedures (see above and McPherson and Raffe (1978))

leavers with 'negative' attitudes to their schooling are likely to have been undersampled; the net effect is to bias the returns towards a slightly more optimistic picture than would emerge from a consideration of all leavers

ii) arising from non-response to the surveys

as above

iii) arising from non-response to the invitation to write open-ended comments

no discernible bias with respect to non-certificate leavers; small tendency for disgruntled O grade and Highers leavers to comment more often

iv) arising from individual unreliability

individual reliability was high among non-certificate leavers with respect to reports of truancy; any individual unreliability is of doubtful relevance to assessments of the experience of the sample

v) arising from the nature of the invitation to write open-ended comments

although those who commented were broadly representative (see i-iii), the possibility that, within each comment, writers chose to mention 'negative' aspects of the schooling they had experienced more often than

	the positive aspects cannot logically be excluded. Neither can the converse logically be excluded. Evidence internal to the data suggests that any bias may not be major but this evidence is not conclusive. It should be noted that distributions on fixed-alternative items (Tables 2-6) largely accord with impressions formed from the open-ended writings
vi) arising from the stage of the leavers' lives at which they were surveyed	no discernible bias; the idea of bias is of doubtful relevance in this context
vii) arising from the stage the school system had reached in the mid seventies	the idea of bias is of doubtful relevance.

We may conclude that the leavers' writings that were obtained were a reasonably representative sample of the writings that would have been obtained from all leavers, had they been successfully approached, the effect of such biases as there were towards 'negative experiences' being counteracted by opposite biases earlier in the surveying procedure. There is no obvious bias associated with the method of approach though there may be other shortcomings (*eg* resulting in inexplicit writing) and advantages (*eg* resulting in more considered writing).

Where we are interested *per se* in the views of recent school leavers it is doubtfully relevant to ask whether their responses are typical of other past or future pupils or of themselves or an earlier stage in their career. Hence questions of bias do not arise. Nor do they arise in relation to the two questions of whether the respondents views are a representative sample, first, of views of the 'real' situation or, second, of all possible views. They are neither of these, and they do not pretend to be. The views, say, of inspectors, teachers, or administrators, may be quite different, and so may those of politicians and parents. The 'bias' of a sample of views can only be established in relation to an authoritatively identified population of views. Though some may think that they have an unimpeachable authority to decree what is the 'real' situation, and what is, therefore, the correct population of views on that situation, such an authority does not reside in the position of inspector or administrator, of pupil or teacher, of parent or politician. Nor does it reside in the position of social scientist or university researcher. The authority emerges, and this is a point to which we shall return, from a process in which all voices are heard, including those of the pupils themselves.

How was the selection of writings made?

One person, Lesley Gow, read all of the accounts returned by respondents to the 1979 survey and a random thousand of those returned in the 1977 survey. She also used a content-analysis of themes in the 1977 writings. This analysis had earlier been conducted by Edith Cope and John Gray. What came out from these two overviews was a picture of an educational landscape that resembled the more systematic mapping that was emerging at the same time from the analyses of the fixed-alternative questionnaire items that were being conducted both by other researchers in the CES team, and by outsiders. The selection of writings was then

made using primarily literary criteria, in order to realise or 're-present' this picture
to the general reader.

Several arguments justify the freedom we have taken in making our selection in
this way. First, we have been able to show that the large number of accounts that
were studied were broadly representative in a number of senses. Indeed we have
laboured at some length the point that our method has systematically gathered
accounts from all parts of the educational scene as it was experienced by pupils.
Hence, though our understanding of what is urgent or important is, inevitably, a
personal response, it is at least a response to the whole landscape. Our choices
have, moreover, been guided by the general correspondence between the content
of the leavers' accounts and what the quantitative analyses seemed to be saying.
Also, we saw little point in pretending that an edited set of writings was anything
other than a literary product which, if it were to succeed, must achieve its effects in
its own terms. But, of course, in representing a landscape one perceives selectively
and interprets one's perceptions. It is therefore as well for us to try to be as explicit
as we can about how we have done this. In particular we must explain why we
chose to present the picture largely through the eyes and the experience of the non-
certificate leaver and of leavers on the 'fringes' of the certification system (see
Table 1 in Appendix).

A number of considerations influenced us. As we have already seen, non-
certificate leavers more often had something extra to say; and they were evidently
more concerned that their voices should be heard. To some extent this may have
resulted from the fact that they had received a shorter questionnaire than had O
grade leavers or Highers leavers. On the other hand, we may conjecture that, other
things being equal, the completion of a questionnaire and the appending of further
comments demanded more of the average non-certificate leaver than of, say, the
average O grade leaver. And yet, both in 1977 and 1979, the former were about as
likely to reply to the questionnaire and were more likely to add comments
(Appendix, Table 8). We took this as a further indication of the urgency that was
apparent in many of the non-certificate writings, an urgency that moved
respondents to write despite the obvious difficulty or diffidence that many felt in
using the written word. Despite such difficulties, however, and despite the fact
that the writings of especially the Highers leavers tended to be longer, the non-
certificate writings in general had qualities of insight, vigour and expression that
the others lacked. These qualities had often, doubtless, been evoked by the
experience of failure and rejection that had characterised the later secondary
schooling of so many non-certificate pupils. In a sense, therefore, a bias is
introduced when we respond to the literary qualities in these writings for the good
and readable work may often have been produced by pupils who had reason to
have strong feelings on the matters about which they wrote or who had
experienced education from what may be, to many of us, new and unusual
perspectives. The dilemma here would appear to be intractable in that we would,
presumably, want and expect these very qualities—of insight, vigour, expression
and feeling—also to be apparent in the writings of pupils who had experienced
success in their education. And yet generally they were not.

In the 1979 Survey, when they were given as full a prompt as the non-certificate
leavers, half the Highers respondents added comments. Some of the best of these
are included in the final chapter of the book. But the following illustrate the way in
which academically successful leavers tended to respond:

'I find that all my subjects inter-relate with my present course. I find the least useful subject Maths, and the most useful English. CSYS was good because it helped me to work on my own, however my teachers were very unhelpful in obtaining books, which they had previously promised to do. Our prelims were sat in Nov. which I found good because we could rest over Christmas. I found doing extra 'O' grades *very* helpful and extremely interesting & *very easy*. I wish however I had taken H Economics, as it is involved in my course now. I would advise all students to take O grades in the subjects they intend to study at University.'

'I feel that the subjects taught at school are of little relevance to what I am doing now. I think the idea of an exam at the end of the last year, covering a wide variety of subjects would be of more help than sitting various subjects. I realized too late that some of the subjects I studied I was not interested in and it was either too late or impossible for me to change to other subjects. I also feel that I anyway would get on a lot better if my general knowledge was improved. In any of the interviews I attended it was always general knowledge questions I was asked.'

In other words, Highers leavers tended to write about the detail of the curricula and examinations that had largely occupied their time for each of the previous two or three years; and the same was also true of the more successful O grade leavers. Success appears to have inhibited the readiness or ability to write more generally about the meaning and purpose of their education. Perhaps this reflects on the questions we asked; perhaps it is a reflection on the present criteria of success in education. Either way, a long selection of such writings would have been dull indeed.

Two further considerations influenced our decision to concentrate primarily on the experience and writings of non-certificate leavers. First, routinely produced official statistics that tell us something about the state of education have in the past mainly described pupils and leavers who obtained publicly recognised qualifications. This restriction resulted partly from the preoccupation of educational policy-makers in the 'fifties and 'sixties with the production of skilled manpower and partly from the belief that the practical problems of collecting usable data from and about less able pupils did not justify the expense. However, building on earlier work in the 'sixties by the Scottish Education Department, which pioneered the regular administration of a postal survey to qualified school leavers, the Centre's surveys in the 'seventies have overcome some of the practical difficulties of surveying all types of school-leaver, whether or not they have academic qualifications. Among other expedients it has proved necessary to use a shorter questionnaire for non-certificate leavers. Hence our present focus on the non-certificate story is intended partly to compensate for the limitations of the quantitative information that is available about these leavers. It may also do something to redress any imbalance in the public understanding of the state of the education system that has arisen from the fact that it has hitherto tended to be the more successful pupils who have figured in the routinely-produced public account (McPherson and Raffe 1978).

Our choice of writings has also been influenced by the response of teachers, administrators, college lecturers and others to the small selections of leavers' writings from the 1977 survey that have been published twice yearly in the *Collaborative Research Newsletter* in a section called 'Pupil Voices'. This has mainly reproduced the comments of non-certificate leavers and of those with low qualifications in the O grade. The *Newsletter* is distributed by the CES to all post-primary educational institutions in Scotland and it carries articles and reports on the programme of Collaborative Research that has been funded in the CES by the Social Science Research Council since 1975. Through this programme educationists from all over Scotland and elsewhere have been able to play a full part in the planning and analysis of the CES surveys of school leavers. Much of this work has concerned the quantifiable data from the fixed-alternative survey questions. These have been placed in the Scottish Education Data Archive (SEDA) that is administered by the Centre. The data are available to anyone with an interest in education, provided they observe the Code of Practice that governs their use (Centre for Educational Sociology 1979). Many users of the SEDA, (of whom there are now over four hundred), and many readers of the Newsletters that carry some of the results of their work, have told us that the 'Pupil Voices' are a valuable additional source of information and insight and that more of them should be made available, and made available more widely. The feeling has been that the accounts of the less able leavers often vividly express important aspects of their school experience that are less easily conveyed to a wider public through the more standardised medium of fixed-alternative questions.

Altogether the writings of some four thousand respondents were studied, all but one thousand of them being from the 1979 Survey. A little under four hundred have been selected for publication. Of these two thirds had been returned by non-certificate leavers, a quarter by those achieving only D or E grades in the SCE O grade, and a tenth by those with better academic qualifications. Within each theme, the main criteria of selection were literary, in two senses. We looked first to the intrinsic quality of each passage of writing. But we were also concerned, second, with the cumulative impact of the selection. Hence certain passages were included primarily because they made for continuity, contrast, emphasis, relief or other effects. We have included too some passages whose effects were not fully under their authors' control. In this respect we also decided to leave, unchanged, idiosyncracies of spelling, punctuation, syntax and expression on the grounds that they may sometimes assist the readers' interpretation of what the writer is trying to communicate. On occasion it is a pity that we cannot reproduce the actual writing. It is also a pity that respect for individual anonymity prevents our appending to each story more of the detail of the individual's life as recorded in the questionnaire. Only the barest facts are given and details have sometimes been altered where anonymity might otherwise have been compromised.

The criteria for selection were not solely literary. We have included too, some writing that fills out the picture of the educational and working lives of academically less qualified leavers. Overall, the frequency and urgency with which non-certificate leavers wrote about different aspects of their experience more or less gave us the broad framework: selection and rejection; truancy; discipline and corporal punishment; curriculum and relationships; working life and unemployment. These were the things that were important to them in the context of the questionnaire. But within this framework we have tried also to cover examples of good and bad practice, responses to available forms of educational provision (such as subjects, link courses and work experience schemes) and, where we could find them, instances of enthusiasm, happiness or pleasure. The first six chapters are based mainly on the writings of the non-certificate leavers, those who were presented for no SCE examinations whilst at school. Also included in these are accounts by pupils on the fringes of the certification system at school or after, namely those who had achieved no A–C awards in the SCE O grade examination.

Together these groups comprised just under half of all leavers in the later seventies. Only the final chapter carries the writing of leavers who had done better than this academically.

In several respects, therefore, our procedures for selection have introduced a conscious bias into the collection that follows. To risk labouring the pictorial metaphor it is not so much that we have ignored certain areas in the selection we have made; discerning readers should find, somewhere in the collection, at least a sketchy depiction of most of the features with which they are familiar. Nevertheless, it is true that we have applied the paint more richly in some areas than in others; and, as we have argued, inevitably so, in view of the varying quality and quantity of the raw materials which we were able to use. What we have tried to communicate with this selection is our understanding of the vivid and urgent stories that are told by a representative sample of Scottish school leavers who were using a medium that, we believe, did not introduce serious biases into their accounts. Whether other editors would have made a different selection, reproducing a different picture, we cannot say; but we do at least know that ours accords with and amplifies the understanding that a number of groups and individuals have reached in their analyses of the survey data in the SEDA. And the beauty of the SEDA data is that, unlike the more confidential writings or autobiographies, they are available for public scrutiny, re-working and development. Judgements based on the SEDA are therefore less likely to be irretrievably arbitrary than are those based on a selection of individual statements. But there is surely room for both sorts of evidence.

How can we achieve better understanding and better practice?

As we have explained, whilst we think these leavers' accounts are honest, we do not believe that they necessarily tell *the* truth about any of the situations they describe. Indeed, it is easy enough to show that the accounts are often incomplete and in consequence apportion responsibility unevenly. In the leavers' eyes, for example, teachers bear the brunt of the blame and win most of the praise that is going, and this is understandable enough. But most of the agencies that play some part in the making of educational policy and practice appear only fleetingly as shadowy figures in the accounts of one or two pupils. References to 'politicians', to 'the government', to 'beurocrats', to the 'Board' or to 'the English' are few and far between, and school inspectors, and advisers (would they welcome this or not?) merit not one mention. But if we cannot look to pupils themselves for an explanation and a remedy, where can we look? Many of them, after all, are looking to someone in the adult world: 'I think you should try more to help us . . instead of just talking a lot of rubbish all the time to us saying you's will help but you's dont. And I think you's have got a cheek asking me to fill this in after all you's should have came and told us what to do for the best instead off asking kids lots of things to help other people'. Which of us is confident that we could meet this demand and supply an answer to the plea that lies behind it for an authoritative interpretation that will sustain action 'for the best'? If we cannot, can we really reject pupils' and leavers' views as hopelessly ill-informed, biased and incomplete? Our own view is that better interpretations can only emerge from public dialogue in which all viewpoints can be heard and all actions and beliefs are open to critical scrutiny. We have tried in recent years to incorporate this view into the conduct of our own research, by offering to educationists throughout Scotland both a real opportunity to influence the content of our regular surveys of school leavers and also a real opportunity to analyse the results of these surveys and apply them to the areas with which they are concerned. (More detail of these opportunities is given in the Appendix). In this way many practitioners who would not ordinarily have had access to the 'big science' of survey research and computers have been able to discuss topics publicly on the basis of research evidence. And in this way too, we have been encouraged to extend the coverage of our surveys, which had earlier been limited to 'qualified school leavers', to include leavers of all types. Participants in our research have included teachers, inspectors, administrators, careers officers, lecturers and others (McPherson, Raab and Raffe 1978). But how is the pupil's voice to be heard and how are pupils to be helped to speak advisedly? How can they be assisted to a better understanding of the part that the education system plays in people's lives and of the part that pupils themselves play in the education system? Something can be done of course with analyses of pupils' responses to pre-structured questionnaires and with discussions of their open-ended writings. But, unless such aids to understanding are also made available to pupils themselves, their experience is bound to remain fragmented and incompletely understood, controlled and expressed.

We have, therefore, two reasons for taking the pupil voice seriously. First, it is a dangerous practice to proscribe categories of evidence, to treat as inconsequential the reaction of any person to what we do. Second, helping the pupil to speak and understand, to reflect on experience, to locate it in wider contexts and set it against other examples, is surely in itself an educational enterprise. If we are reluctant to listen to pupils and engage them in dialogue, then we are almost certainly also reluctant to educate them. And that is exactly what many pupils say is the case.

For this reason we would hope to see increasing use of the SEDA and of this collection of writings in, among other places, the schools themselves. We can envisage a variety of ways in which these two resources, and ones like them, might be used, either singly or in combination. First, the writings could play a part, perhaps through the medium of guidance and of social education, in helping the pupils to think about the outlines and trajectory of their emerging school career. Using the accounts, pupils could ask 'who am I like; what has been happening to pupils like me in the recent past?' and so on. Class discussion and creative writing could also contribute here. Opinions could be polled and statistical summaries prepared, both numerical and visual. Thinking about identity and career might in its turn lead to wider considerations: for example, what is the structure of occupations and of education and training for school leavers; how did it develop; how does it vary from one part of the country to another? Such questions take one to the areas of geography, modern studies and economics, and some of them can be illuminated by statistical analyses of the SEDA. Thus an element of computer appreciation and computer studies might also be introduced at this point. There is no reason in principle why schools and pupils should not run their own analyses of the data produced by leavers' surveys from as far back as 1962 that are stored in the SEDA. The operations are technically simple; a self-instruction course has already been prepared (Gray and McPherson 1979) and many beginners have successfully mastered the rudiments, among them school leavers themselves.

In these and other ways, the experience of schooling could itself become part of an integrated course that could be entered at a variety of levels and for a variety of purposes both cognitive and affective. The overriding purpose would be to help pupils to a fuller understanding of how others' lives and their own unfold. Of course, it is notoriously difficult to translate curricular ideas into practice, and perhaps especially so in the case of proposals that allow scope for pupils' views and for critical discussion of the forces that shape their world. But there are advantages to be won. As one fourteen-year-old comprehensive school boy in Edinburgh recently told us, 'My best teachers are the ones who recognise that there's something wrong'. Perhaps it is through the changes we must make in ourselves, in order to acknowledge that the views of all pupils are important, that the beginnings of an answer are to be found.

CHAPTER TWO

'FLUNG ASIDE, FORGOTEN CHILDREN'

Non-certificate classes and pupils

I didn't like my last year at school because the teachers were only interested in the people who were taking O levels, so me and the rest of the people who were not sitting O-levels were more or less flung aside.

Girl, non-certificate. Clothes machinist.

Dear Sir
I was a girl that was not very good at my work. We were all put into a group and forgoten. there was no hope for us. but there is we can all work. My two little sisters are the same. (forgoten children) Help them please. they need help I hope they can do something for them.
Why do all the onces at 20–40 get a job so easily? As I have been interviewed by millions of people and not yet got a job. We school leavers all have to started somewhere just like other people.

(School. Forgoten children)

Girl, non-certificate. Unemployed.

'. . . me and the rest of the people who were not sitting O-levels were more or less flung aside'; 'we were all put into a group and forgotten. . .'. The one feeling that was, perhaps, expressed most strongly and most frequently by any group of leavers writing about their own experience was a bitter sense of rejection among non-certificate boys and girls at their exclusion from certificate course work. There were, as we shall see, 'ones who can sit there O grades and ones who can't', and accompanying this distinction were differences in the care and resources the school was felt to provide and in the respect with which pupils felt they were treated: 'What I did not like about my school was they did not care what you done'; this was all that one pupil, afterwards a metal sorter, had to say about his secondary education. But, even in its brevity, it nevertheless comes close to saying it all.

It is probably little consolation to such pupils that what they felt to be the indignity of their situation has, if anything, been made more acute as a result of the state's attempts in the last fifteen years to extend access to education. During the 1960's the two major political parties in Scotland supported both the raising of the school leaving age to sixteen years (ROSLA) and the principle of comprehensive education. But the abolition of selection at 12 years, the age of transfer in Scotland, has postponed academic selection rather than removed it. Moreover, selection now occurs in a context in which its consequences are more evident, affecting as they do all pupils in the community of each school; and selection now follows the introductory two years of secondary education during the greater part of which a norm of equality of treatment, and even of opportunity, has been at least implicit in the mixed ability organisation of much of the teaching.

Scottish pupils commonly start their O grade course work near the beginning of the third secondary year. Hence in the case of all but those pupils who leave before the O grade examination, the school must live for a further two full sessions with the consequences of the differentiation that is first formalised at this point. Twenty or twenty five years ago the choice of subjects for certificate course work commonly started a year later and at an age when, with a minimum leaving age of fifteen, early leaving had already removed from school the main element that now feels it suffers from invidious comparisons and differentiated treatment. In those days, furthermore, it is likely that, by the age of fourteen more pupils would already have tailored their hopes and expectations to the possibilities that had been opened or closed to them when they were allocated at twelve years of age to a three year or a five year course and, with it, most commonly, to a three year (junior secondary) or five year (senior secondary) school. (The junior secondary school corresponded roughly to the English secondary modern school whilst the senior secondary school resembled the English grammar school. The grammar school, however, was commonly attended by a much smaller proportion of all pupils in compulsory education than was the case with the senior secondary school in Scotland.) When transfer to secondary school was selective it is also likely that any subsequent differentiation of treatment between pupils would have been less visible to pupils themselves for the bulk of them were already in differentiated schools. (In 1965 about one in three of Scottish secondary pupils attended fully 'comprehensive' schools, but even in these the type of course had been largely determined from the first year onwards by the transfer examination and procedures (SED, 1966, Table A)).

What comes through, then, from the early accounts in this section is a strong sense of resentment at what was felt to be inferior treatment where equal treatment had been looked for, an inferior treatment that was compounded by what some pupils thought was the unfair labelling of their abilities, and aggravated by the group reaction of other rejected pupils: '. . . I was put into a class entitled May leavers, It consisted of pupils who were not sitting exams so instead of trying to help us they put us all together and formed what they called ML and what we called Rowdies. Once in this class there was nothing you could do. . .'

But, if exclusion from certificate work precipitated inequalities of treatment and created situations in which pupils felt it difficult to try, whether for reasons of teacher prejudice ('once you're down you stay down') or of group pressure or behaviour ('. . . if there was no such thing as a remedial class, then there would have been no such thing as the common thicky'), it is, nevertheless, far from clear that the universal provision of certificate courses of the present type would have improved matters.

'Maybe I didn't get any O grades but. . .' introduces two consecutive sections of accounts mainly by leavers who had sat at least one SCE O grade but who had failed to achieve any A–C awards (known as passes before 1973). As Table 1 in the Appendix shows, about 14 per cent of all leavers could in this (ultimately arbitrary) sense be regarded as pupils whose experience was marginal to that of other O grade leavers and to that of the non-certificate leavers. Nevertheless, in terms of the then current forms and standards of provision, there were almost as many such pupils as, for instance, there were pupils who passed three or more Highers, a level commonly regarded as a threshold qualification for entry to advanced post-school education (Appendix, Table 1). It is clear enough from the accounts of the marginal certificate pupils that, compared with their non-certificate work, certificate classes were, on the whole, seen as more purposefully organised, and in that sense were felt to have created a context through which teachers could express concern about their pupils ('. . . the more O grades you were sitting, the more interested the teachers were in helping you'). But some pupils found this concern overwhelming: 'All you got told about was your O grades, how hard they were and how we'd have to stick in'.

For almost a hundred years now, since the inception of the Leaving Certificate, Scottish teachers have been relatively reluctant to debar from presentation pupils who have a reasonable chance of success in public examinations. In the sixties and early seventies, indeed, the schools came to present almost seventy per cent of the age group for an O grade examination that had been intended, when it was introduced in 1962, for the most able 30–35 per cent of pupils. Whilst curricular arguments ebbed and flowed as to the appropriate balance between vocational, academic and other subjects, between examinable and non-examinable subjects, and between any sort of conventional subject as against a more 'integrated' curriculum, the major curriculum decisions were being taken by default through school practice in the presentation of pupils for the SCE O grade. And, with the exception of one or two Regions in the later seventies, the 'English solution' to the problem of providing attractive courses for less able pupils, the CSE Mode III, was eschewed in Scotland. Since the standard of the SCE O grade examination has not been greatly changed, if at all, in response to the growing demand for certification, this has meant that, for the majority of O grade pupils, (those presenting only for the O grade and not for the H grade), their school experience has been predominantly one of failure. Among leavers in 1975/6 71 per cent of such pupils failed to achieve a C award or better in at least half the subjects they sat. Moreover many more subjects will have been discontinued as a result of the 'prelims' and other examinations or tests that were taken during the two year course leading up to presentation for the O grade.[1] Whatever the success of current proposals to develop improved (Foundation) courses for non-certificate pupils along the lines first recommended by the Munn and Dunning Committees, the problem of the relation of such courses to the SCE O grade courses (for which major changes are not proposed at the time of writing) will still remain. Moreover, the difficult decision that the schools must make on the course allocation of pupils extends far beyond the fourteen per cent of leavers who gain no A–C awards, in one direction to those who are capable of achieving one or two and, in the other direction, to those with more remote possibilities of success in any O grade attempt.

In view of the established nature of much of the O grade curriculum, decisions on course allocation tend also to be decisions about curriculum. What strikes one, in the two sections of writing by the marginal certificate leavers, is the omission, except in one or two instances, of accounts of the intrinsic attractions, or even utility, of their subjects. Their courses were judged primarily in terms of the consequent attention of teachers and of their (mixed) experience of the value of O grades for finding a job. These were also the main criteria that were used by non-certificate leavers in the suggestions they made for improvements in the curriculum for the last two years of compulsory education, suggestions that are collated in later sections (see '"I liked being at school because . . .": subjects and courses' below).

One outcome that was originally intended for ROSLA was to ensure both that a national examination was available to all pupils (subject to ability) during the period of compulsory schooling and also that compulsory schooling could terminate with that examination. For various reasons about one in ten pupils left school at Christmas either before the possibility of presentation for the SCE or, on occasion, after it. Some of these pupils in the section on 'Christmas leavers' felt that their school had failed to provide for pupils whose age did not fit the organisational convenience of the school year. Others felt that the school was glad of the opportunity created by the possibility of Christmas leaving to encourage them to leave 'early'. In this sense Christmas leaving played a part in the continuous process of selection that is similar to that played, though to much greater effect, by early leaving before ROSLA in 1972. But by retaining other pupils who felt that they had completed all that they could usefully complete at school, Christmas leaving also aggravated discontent and further strained the resources that were already stretched by ROSLA.

Resource difficulties were of course the main reason why ROSLA was several times postponed. In judging the accounts of the 'forgotten children', the reader will no doubt want to recall that these leavers had started their secondary education at or in the immediate aftermath of ROSLA; and they were to continue and complete it in years of teacher shortage, teacher strikes, and part-time education for many. The concluding section '"not very many teachers to teach us": who suffered when teachers and their time was scarce?' is perhaps a timely reminder of the difficulties that face schools in periods of restricted public spending, and it supplies its own answer: 'My last year at school wasn't much use as at that time our school was on part time Education and the school was short staffed we were more or less spent our time sitting ourselves, in classrooms or in the Cloakroom. I did not like that at all. The teachers done their best but that wasn't much help we all wanted to leave and look for work, some teachers even told us although not in so many words that

[1] See Dickson (1979) and Bibby and Weston (1980) for estimates relating to mathematics, languages and sciences and Ballantyne and Taylor (1979) for estimates relating to all SCE O grade attempts.

we were all just wasting our time and their time. I think I stopped going to school about October and Nobody bothered at all . . .'. The tacit collusion of some teachers in the seeming worthlessness of the final year for non-certificate pupils is symptomatic of the bankruptcy of the case on which the school system has hitherto based its power and authority over older pupils. 'Certification for employment' carries some conviction in relation to more able pupils and in times of full employment; and it is the inspiration on which much of policy for curriculum and further education in Scotland has been based since the mid fifties. But it carries less conviction when youth unemployment is high and less conviction for those pupils whose publicly accredited attainments, if any at all, will place them at the bottom of the hierarchy of leavers that is competing for positions. In this sense the greatest resource that the schools at present lack is a universally acknowledged justification for the compulsion that they exercise over pupils. Many pupils and apparently some teachers recognise that the schools' current claims to legitimacy cannot, in their nature, be extended over all pupils. In a universal system of hierarchical certification some leavers will find themselves at the bottom of the ladder. In a system where certification is traded for jobs, and where jobs are scarce, those at the bottom will have most difficulty in finding work and most cause to be sceptical about school. If the school is to be able to 'bother' about the pupil who disappears in his or her final compulsory year it must be on some basis that, in the words of the Scottish Advisory Council on Education in 1947, 'postulates equal care for the education of all boys and girls up to eighteen years of age' (SED 1947, para 24).

Under a quarter of non-certificate boys and girls thought that their last year at school was 'worthwhile' (Appendix, Table 2) and they thought this largely independently of whether they were in employment when they completed the questionnaire. Under half the non-certificate leavers 'enjoyed' their last year (Appendix, Table 3). By contrast, over half the O grade leavers thought their last year had been worthwhile and almost seven out of ten said they had enjoyed it. In a quarter of schools the percentage of all leavers, whatever their qualifications, who thought their last year 'worthwhile' was not more than 36 per cent in each school. In a quarter of schools the percentage of all leavers who said they had enjoyed their last year was not more than 49 per cent in each school (Appendix, Table 7). These figures give us a framework within which to assess the accounts that follow.

'One's who can sit there 'O' grades and one's who cant'
what non-certificate pupils thought about non-certificate classes

At our school we were put into groups one's who can sit there 'O' grades and one's who can't which is unfair. The one's who did not sit there 'O' Grades the teachers never Botherd to learn them anything. The only Good thing about the school was p.e. as that was the only class the teachers Bothered about us. The one's who were not in 'O' grade classes never got to see anybody about a job for advice so no wonder pupils stade off as much.

Girl, non-certificate. Apprentice book binder.

I was in a none certificate cours at school, so the last year at school was boring. The teachers could have made the time more useful by showing more interest in what they were teaching us. Some teachers leave you in the class room to get on with your work, so if theres a question you dont no you have to leave it until the teacher comes back, but by the time he or she chose the period is over, so you dont get to know how to do the question. And the same happens the next day and so on. In this pameflit you ask what you did at school, In question 5 I tell you I would like to have been better at Maths and English, and been abel to speek a foreign language. Well to go to night school it would cost to much.

Boy, non-certificate. Apprentice welder.

I didn't like the way a lot of the teacher's ignored us, well our two classes that were not 'O' grade classes. They always reminded us about not taking O grades, and how hard it would be for the ones who didn't take O grades to get jobs. But in the factory that I work there are some girls I know from school who took there O grades and passed them but still ended up as ordinary factory worker's. When teachers at school urged them to take O grades and they would all end up with good jobs and professions. Teachers would have made the time more useful by not preaching about O grades and talking about work and the future. My job I would say is reasonable and happy work and I get on well with the people I mainly work with, which I suppose really matters to have a happy job and to be happy at your work.

Girl, non-certificate. Sewing machinist.

As I have no O levels there was no point in doing the last yr of school, and I got the feeling from the teacher that as I was in my last yr at school. They did not bother with my class very much. We were just put there in the class to keep us from roaming the street and maybe getting into trouble, so I dont see any point in staying on.
I am now 17 yrs of age and at first found it difficult to find a job. I was very lucky to have now found one which I now enjoy doing. As you know from the last page my mother is a widow. The wages I am getting now are £26 pa. That is not to bad but I would like to have got a job where the money is bigger. But my mother helps me a lot and I do enjoy the work and I will have a trade to look forward to.

Boy, non-certificate. Trainee stock controller.

I liked my last year at school because if you weren't sitting O levels you didn't have to go to school. I didn't like maths at school. If you had to go to school, they would have made it useful for you by giving you work to do and trying to make you understand and do things if you couldn't.

Girl, non-certificate. Assembly line worker.

I did not like my last year at school at all. Those who were doing a non-certificate course were asked to sit in a class with a book opened at any page at all and pretend to be reading in case the head-master or someone like that would come into the room. If you were not interested in O-levels then the teachers couldn't be bothered with you.

Girl, non-certificate. In part-time job.

In my last year at school I was in a class which wasn't sitting 'O' levels. The reason for me being in that class was because I didn't get a good mark for my 1st year French Exam so I was put into that non 'O' grade class. The only thing I didn't like at school was a few teachers. I think the teachers could have learnt the class I was in a lot more than they did when I was in my 3rd year some teachers couldn't be bothered teaching the class anything so they told us to play cards in the classroom or go outside to play football. Some teachers didn't like our class behaviour I dont blame them but if they hadn't put us in a non 'O' Grade class they couldn't behave like this in class.

Boy, non-certificate. Apprentice turner.

In my last year at school wasn't worthwhile. As the teachers had no time for you. I never got the chance to sit any O-levels, because only so many were allowed. I think the (_____ High) should let everybody sit them. My cousin is in her third year and she has not got the chance either. Some teachers I liked but others had no time for you. My English teacher did not do much writing with us it was always reading. As for maths I hated that because they gave you stupid adding up sums that they do in Primary schools. The book is called Simple Arithmetic. I hope you can help the people that do not have a chance sitting O-levels.

Girl, non-certificate. Assembly factory worker.

I didn't like school as it is biased towards the intelligent people and didn't always try to help the people who were not so intelligent. The best teachers are always given to the best classes and teachers who taught the lower classes couldn't always teach them very well.
At job interviews preference is always given to the people with qualifications. Even though some are good at manual work they are ignored because they weren't good at academic work.

Boy, non-certificate. On a work experience scheme as a labourer.

I was in a none O level class in my last two years at school and I could kill myself now because I was well warned, by my parents and my brother and sister told me their mistakes but because I was in a none O level class I sometime felt that the teacher's just didn't bother enough, as myself I liked sewing very much but when you asked this teacher anything which I had she always has the same excuse. Well I think some people in a none O level class and want to learn what they like but I felt that you were pushed about. At the moment I'm in a very good job and I count myself very lucky to have a job that I'm happy in and I have two very good bosses and every day I'm learning because I went into this job knowing nothing. Well thank you very much and I hope any information that I have given might help some school leaver that think leaving school will be good because it hits you very hard not having a job to go to.

Girl, non-certificate. Office junior.

In my last year at school I wasnt sitting any O levels and the teachers didn't bother if you went to school or not. All they were worried about was the O level people. No wonder so many people played truant because they don't get enough attention from their teachers.

Girl, non-certificate. Textile machinist.

I only liked being with Friend at School. I did not like the teachers. the work I got at school was so easy you did not learn eny thing like the other fourth years learnt. it was the same work we got over and over again for I was in l low glass in first and second year and then buy the time I went into Fourth year we never don hardly any work. We never got home work after first year. And I have leaned more in the year I left school than I ever did at school by going out and doing them.

Girl, non-certificate. Works in a sweet factory.

What i did not like about my school was that they did not care what you done.

Boy, non-certificate. Metal sorter.

My friend and I took school as a big joke as we all had jobs to go to. I lost interest in the last year. The thing I did not like about the school was lot of the teachers if you were in a high class you were treated better and spoke to better & if you were in a low class you were treated like dirt.

Girl, non-certificate. Apprentice florist.

'What they called the May leavers and we called the Rowdies'
pupils' views on selection and differentiation, and how they reacted

When I was at school I was known as one of the class rowdies after your second year teachers didn't want to know you because they couldn't handle you. My last year at school I was put into a class entitled May leavers. It consisted of pupils who were not sitting exams so instead of trying to help us they put us all together and formed what they called M.L. and what we called the Rowdies.
Once in this class there was nothing you could do you coudln't start behaing because you were branded and that was you teachers just didn't want to know you.

Boy, non-certificate. Van boy.

Teachers could make it more usefull by treating us with more respect than just the common thicky. They could have also got rid of the remedial classes for these people are intelligent but just never got the chance to prove

themselves. I was one but I got an
understanding teacher and he gave me a chance
so I was moved into an O level english class but
I was ignored because I was remedial. Pretty
soon I was back in my old class not because I
could not do the work but because of the
atmosphere that was set of by the other pupils.
So you see, if there was no such thing as a
remedial class, then there would have been no
such thing as the common thicky.
Boy, non-certificate. Employment unknown.

While in school I was treated like an idiot not
only by the teachers but by my headmaster. I
was not given any chance to show my own
potential because the class I was in did not give
or have the brains (as my headmaster would
say) to know that qualifications are an essential
for good employment. I got stuck in at my
work and showed great interest but knowing the
teachers in my school, the supposedly clever
ones got all their attention. I myself am not
very good at expressing myself, but if you only
knew the torment it gave me knowing I would
have put every effort into being given the
chance to sit O level, andyet ones in the O level
class did not give two hoots about school
altogether.
*Boy. O grades, no A–C awards, Went
straight from school to a full-time course at an
FE College.*

I have a steady job. Ive never regreted leaving
school. I had a job waiting through all my last
year of School, so I feel my last year of School
was totally useless, it just waisted a whole year
of my life. What I didnt like was the setting of
the periods. But the best thing about the School
was the activaties at the end of the week. One
thing about the teachers, though, I think they
should not be able to put someone out of a O
grade O level, ect it should be thourghly
checked eg your work looked over by the
Authorities.
*Boy. O grades, no A–C awards. Apprentice
painter.*

I want to see in later education, pupils and
Teachers being a sort of family. When I was at
school my teachers made me feel thick really
stupid so I did not bother to study, they made
me feel as if it was not worth my while thinking
of what I wanted to be. I had my heart set on
being a child nurse but I have no confidence in
my self anymore so I shall never forget my
teachers and how they made me feel. I hope
when I have my children they will be
encouraged as I dont want them to be hurt like
me. I dont think my teachers meant to be like
this. but if they had encouraged me I would

have went to college or something but I started
to skip school and not study. But they
encouraged the more brighter girls to go on and
be what they wanted to be. I hope I have been
helpful and I will help in any further questions
if necessary. One more point the brighter pupils
should be aloud to help the not so bright pupils
and teachers should pay more attention to the
not so bright because they seem to ignore us.
Girl. O grades, no A–C awards. Shop assistant.

When I was in 1st year I was in a 'A' class the
same in 2nd year. But I played truant with a
friend. (We were both in the same class) when
caught her mother came to school kicked a fuss.
By the way, Mother is very well known, for
charity work, church work all that, and is rather
a snob. Well I was put down a class, and she
was kept where she was (this was going into 3rd
year). Later I wouldn't go to school as the class
I was in well it was filth and nothing else, but I
went and decided to work my way up
(headmaster said, work hard and get your own
standard). I did for about 2 or 3 months
nothing. Science teacher told me 'you won't be
going back up', 'once your down you stay
down'. which was true. Anyway teachers tend
to under estimate pupils. I'm quite intelligent
really but you just don't get a chance to show
what you can do teachers just don't help at all.
It isn't a grudge against anybody it's just I
know, it happened to me. 'A' class is a high
Grade. By-the-way, thank you as well.
Girl, non-certificate. Unemployed.

I don't actually think that anyone should be
able to say what I can do and cant do. When
we were at the _____ school we were told
that we would be able to sit 2 o'grades. When it
came to the first year I studied so that I could
get fairly good marks in my report, and I think
that I did, I got a 'B' pass in English, I failed
an 'A' by ½ a mark, and a B+ in Arithmetic.
these were meant to be the subjects that we
were allowed to sit an o'grade in. But even
although I passed the exam's, the education
did'nt think that it was good enough to sit an
o'grade, so I never got to.
Actually it is a fact that not one person in my
course got to sit an o'grade. That is the thing I
did'nt like, plus the fact after sitting exams in
the last year we never even got a report card.
I am very glad that I got a job in an office, now
I have finished being an office junior and am
now the commissions clerkess, so that I can
sicken the teachers because half of them under
estimate us and think that all we are fit for
doing is working in shops or factories.
Girl, non-certificate. Office junior.

'Maybe I didnt get any O grades but . . .'
were O grades worthwhile for pupils who gained no A–C awards?

I think that what I have learnt at school has been useful. Maybe I didn't get any 'O' Grades except an E in Arithmetic, but, I still have the knowledge of each subject I sat. One of the subject I was was Secetarial Studies this is one that is very useful in my job, at present.

Girl. O grades, no A–C awards. Receptionist/ typist.

I think these days you have to have a lot of O grades + highers to help you get a better than average job. As I have no certificates at all, some of my collegues + workmates have up to 7 O grades and some highers, and they are no different from me, and honestly speaking I am better at my apprenticeship than most, so I *do not* think that the present system of education is much cop or any good, etc. because O grades never did me any good or harm. But they can be very hurting to many very intelligent students. So you can see I am *very much against* O grades Highers etc. in particular. It is very disappointing to see so many people of my age in life, unemployed. I would very much like to see a better standard of education in Scotland.

Boy. O grades, no A–C awards. Apprentice engineer.

When I was attending school it was rather boring, the last year or two all you heard about was 'O' Grades and jobs or staying on at school. The teachers were never really interested in what you thought and what you wanted to do when you left school. By the time you were sitting your 'O' Grades you were sick of hearing about them and gradually being put of them and loosing interest. My new job has made me see things differently now and I am treated better at work no more bossing about from the teachers. I like it better.

Girl. O grades, no A–C awards. Works for a distillers company.

As soon as I left school I got a job right away in a tea factory I have nearly been in a year it is very boring low paid for a factory, and very dirty. I liked most of the teachers at school they were helpful, but I didnt like most of the subjects, I didn't find work hard, but I don't like looking for a job I think it's embarrising. I

think young ones should be encouraged to stay on at school and sit O levels unless they wan't into a factory but I just wish I would have studied more so I could have got a job which was not boring and you got somewhere in life.

Girl. O grades, no A–C awards. Tea packer.

At school I liked most of my subjects and the teachers. Most of the teachers have got patients with you and other haven't. I didn't like spending an hour and 10 mins in one class as 3 to 6 classes were non-certificate and it wasted a lot of time.

Boy. 1 O grade C award. Prawn peeler.

During my last year at school I found it interesting in O level subjects and a complete waste of time in others. I think the age for school leavers should be 15. the present age for school leaving is an easy way of reducing unemployment for the government.

Boy. O grades, no A–C awards. General labourer.

I did like the subjects at scholl but I did not like the teaching techniques ie. myself and several others who were able to do well and grasp a subject quickly recieved most of the attention where as other pupils less adaptable were left more or less to manage on their as best they could.

Girl, non-certificate—the 'attention' she mentions may be explained by the fact that she took at least one CSE examination. Works as a bottling line assistant.

In my last year at school expecially I liked the way teachers changed towards me as they were concerned about your future and told you of the preperation which you had to make for going into the world. But all through school I felt that I was building up to my O'Grades and would be satisfied when I got my results, but it was a big let down when I got them and found that it was not what I had imagined.
My results have effected my choice of jobs greatly, my present job is the one I had before leaving school and was realy only looked upon as something to fall back on if I couldn't get into nursing, but I ended up as the only job I could get.
Abolision of set O'Grade exams would change a lot in the way of young people looking for jobs. General Knowlege of every subject studied in schools from the age of 5 should be the evidence of a person's capability.

Girl. O grades, no A–C awards. Shop assistant.

What I think about school is its a bit of a waste
because you sit all your grades and when I left
school in may I did'nt have my results so got a
Job without them. my job is steady and with a
good future and O grades have'nt done a thing.
*Boy. O grades, no A–C awards. Catering
trainee.*

What I liked best about my school was I had
only a few hundred yards to walk. Therefore I
could arrive quite early and had no bus fares to
pay. One thing I'll always remmember is the
more O grades a pupil was sitting the more
interested the teachers were in helping you. To
help young people who are looking for jobs, I
think there should be more opportunity for
young people not sitting O'grades, as well as
those sitting O'grades who often find jobs a lot
sooner than a young person who has been
thrown to the back of the class and forgotten
about.
*Girl. O grades, no A–C awards. Shop
assistant.*

When I left school I was on the dole for 6
weeks. I was lucky to get a local job the first
day I started I really hated it. You were sat
down a a seat shown once what to do and you
were left to get on with it. When I was at
school I really hated my 3rd and 4th year. All
you got told about was your O Grades, how
hard they were and how wed have to stick in.
Because the teachers spoke about it so much we
got bored listening to it that I gave up caring.
When I was at my last school it was great
because we got on great with the teachers and
they made the lessons more interesting.
I think that sitting O Grades is a waste of time
because it doesn't matter how many you have
you always end up either getting turned down
cause you've got too many or taken on because
you've none.
I didn't like going for interviews because most
of them I had to put the patter on and act
polite in the way I spoke. They should just take
you as they find you. I think before you leave
school that you should be shown round works
and colleges to give you an idea of what your
going to be left to make your mind up to do
when you leave. I hope I've been some help.
Girl. O grades, no A–C awards. Unemployed.

'I didn't really try'
leavers who blamed
themselves for not gaining
A–C awards

Personally, the last year at school for myself
was frightning, the teachers really confused me.
I was afraid of what work was going to be like.
I had no idea of the change it would have on
me. Teachers should treat the kids like adults
the last year, put them at their ease, some of
course won't respond. But, they can try! I'm
not saying they don't. I know now *I* didn't
really try, the last year. I Sincerely hope I've
helped you.
*Boy. O grades, no A–C awards. Shop
assistant.*

I would just like to say that if I could have
started school again I would have studied hard I
liked the way I was treated at school by the
teachers. They didn't treat me like a child I
don't blame the teachers for my failing my
exams it was my own fault.
Just now I am happy in my job I don't intend
staying there all my life. I'm going to start
night school and resit a couple of O'levels.
I think there should be more employers willing
to take on young people. They should at least
let them try.
Well, I hope I've helped you out by answering
these questions.
*Girl. O grades, no A–C awards. Works in a
light engineering workshop.*

I liked schoal my last year becouse we didnt do
any schoal work. most of the time we would
discuss all sorts of things. I can't remember the
parts I didn't like.
I only wish I had stuck in at schoal and got my
'O' grades instead of getting into a
gang + trouble and get expelled.
I wish I could start schoal again, so as I could,
listen to te advice I got from my teachers.
I was lucky in finding work because of the
Careers Office. I don't like my presant job as
there is not a lot of work and I am in an office
by myself.
I think the services supplied do all they can to
find employment for young people.
Thank you.
*Girl. O grades, no A–C awards. Office
worker.*

If I had my chance I would of stayed in school
and learned instead of just mucking around. I
would like to of taken my O' levels as well as

now you can't get a job without O' levels. The work I have its' nothing exciting and now I realies I should of stayed on school longer as I would of had a better job—school was great realy you had your friends and some teachers would have a good laugh with you But once you leave well that's you and you have to started looking for a job which is realy hard. pluse your wages are poor if I have any children their not leaving school they all stay on so they have a good eduction and will get better jobs I wouldn't envy who's leave school it the best time of your life I would go back any day.

Girl. O grades, no A–C awards. On a work experience scheme as a shop assistant.

'So I left the Christmas before O levels'
Christmas leavers

I did not really like anything at school except for gynmastics and swimming. Out of all the teachers at this Secondary School very very few took intrests in their pupils work, personnal Problem; or anything else. I personnaly only knew of one teacher that took an intrest in nearly every thing all her pupils did.
I think more people of all ages should be taken on, in all these job Creation Schemes as I found out it came in very handy, for me and a few friends I know. I was suppose to do 4 O'level subjects but as I did not like school I couldn't wait to leave so I left the Christmas before the O'levels, but now I wish I would have done them.

Girl, non-certificate Christmas leaver. Clerkess.

The school I was at was _____. It was quiet a good school and the teachers are very helpful. When I was at school I took eight O' grade subjects but left before sitting them because I had the chance of a job. The teachers were mad but I wanted to start work.

Boy, non-certificate Christmas leaver.
Apprentice butcher.

I left school at christmas 1977. I was in O' level classes but I didin't stay on to sit them—I wasin't needing O' levels for the 1 was wanted because when I left school I was just wanting to work in a factory I didin't want anything fancy. I am happy in my job at the _____ [clothes] factory. I like my job it was the sort of job I wanted as I like sewing. I wasin't happy in my first job as I didin't like the people they didin't mix with each other at all, but here everybody

talks, and thats what I like.

Girl, non-certificate Christmas leaver, Clothes machinist.

My Second last year at school was very interesting. I tried to work very hard but I wasn't too successful. I got four D passess in my O levels which wasn't very useful. I sat Five O levels my history wasn't even mentioned. I did not really expect it to really. I did not get on with my teacher very well and he didn't like me very much either. Biology I never sat I was hopeless at that. So was everyone else really. I got D passes on Fabric & Fashion, Food & Nutrition, Arithmetic, English. When I left school I was very lucky and got a job right away. I like it very much, the money is good and the girls are nice. The work got boring but I expected that of a factory and I am used to it now.
I left school because I was fed up with it. When they know you are repeating a year they tend to ignore you. The teacher very seldom comes into the class. It is worse when they know you are leaving half way through the year. They group you together and leave you in classrooms for hours and no one comes in. I was glad to leave when I did. I still am. I hope I have helped you.

Girl, non-certificate. Christmas leaver. Clothes machinist.

I was discouraged from staying on at school by some of the teachers. They said I was anti-social and I should leave at Christmas. I was not sixteen till January. therefore I could not get any unemployment payment for over a month. I had no money at all. When I went for interviews they would not concider me because I was only fifteen at that time. I think it is wrong for teachers to be able to tell you to leave school when you are fifteen. I now wish I had been able to stay on at school and finish off the 'O' grade courses I had begun to study. I was taking five 'O' grades and I was going to stay on but opted out of school before the 'O' grades were given out. A lot of my schoolfriends who did not take 'O' grades work beside me but there were in special classes where they got talks from the careers office and had trips to factories etc. while I was studying for 'O' grades. Last year at school was a complete waste of time.

Girl, non-certificate Christmas leaver. Bakery worker.

I liked the friendly atmosphere and the *team* spirit of school. On the whole I loved my schooling and at first I really missed it. When I left I actually went against all my teachers advice they said I should not leave at Christmas but wait till the summer so that I could sit my O grades. But I had no choice my father was ill and as the elder in the family I had to get a job so that he wouldn't work as hard. And I gave up 7 very possible O grades. as my teachers said I had a great chance of passing them. Bit I did get an excellent Schools leaving Certifficate. which has helped me to find work. I think employers should be told that just because someone has not sat O grades or A grades this does not mean they are less intelligent or less willing to do the job. As I think employers tend to want people with qualifications even if they are not required in the *Job.*

Girl, non-certificate Christmas leaver. Stock control clerkess.

I did not like school because the teachers' did not consider the pupils as adult, there were no amenities for even the fourth year pupils.
I left school as soon as I turned sixteen. I would liked to have sat 'O' Grades but this meant that I would have needed to stay on at school for another four months; meanwhile I had the chance to find a job and earn money. Anyway 'O' Grades are not a definite guarantee of acquiring a job.
I hated looking for a job because the Careers Office and Youth Employment offered not advice. Also the prospective employers were very choosy as in this area they can afford to be.

Girl, non-certificate Christmas leaver. Clothes machinist.

What I would really liked to have been was a Nursery Nurse; but teachers were not very helpful in getting information on this. They always seemed as though they were not keen on the idea and made me feel as though I was not capable of sitting 'O' grades and that was why I left school at Christmas, so I felt staying on would have been a waste of time. Since leaving school I started my first job in a boutique but got paid off after a month as there was not enough work. I then started going to the Labour Exchange and was there for 3½ months. Had several interviews 12–18 for jobs. I even tried to get back to school. But the forms they had to fill in for 'O' grades had just been sent away. So I have held my present job since May. This job is very likeable but has nothing to look into the future too.

Girl, non-certificate Christmas leaver. Kitchen assistant.

What I liked about my school was most of the teachers were good to get along with and they would go out of their way to help you. With a

few of the teachers they seems too take an instant disliking too you. For instance if you were asked a question and you didnt tell them the answere they blackmarked you as being lazy, or just stupid. Most of the time in my case, it wasn't that I didn't know the answeres; I *did*, but I was shy and I could never find the words at the right time. What I didn't like was the way all the teachers made me leave at Christmas. They said it was for the best. They talk about educating their pupils, maybe if they paid more attention to the good pupils and ignored all the bad ones, they'd get on better. During my last 2 years of school I was off a lot due to genuine illness. I spent a lot of time in hospital and in bed. But all the time I was off school I really did work hard. I revised for my exams which were coming soon. When I went back too school my teachers had sort of ganged up on me because I'd been off, and they didn't consider letting me try the exams first. They said I'd been off that much that I couldn't possibly pass any of my exams. It was then arranged for my mum too see my house mistress. And it was decided that I would leave. I left but I went too the Tech. College. I could only get into two classes and I went too them—sat my exams—and passed with good results. Therefore I proved them wrong, as I *was* capable of passing my exams. The only thing I found difficult about finding a job was that most employers told me they were looking for over 18's. And as I was only 16 what chance did I stand?

Girl, non-certificate Christmas leaver. Worked as an office junior, on a job creation scheme, before getting a permanent job as a clothes machinist. Sat English, Mathematics and Secretarial Studies O grades at evening classes.

I liked most things except for a couple of subjects and a couple of teachers, although I got on well with most of them. I waited 8 months for a job and I know what it is like trying to get a job, and I feel sorry for those who have still to come through that stage, cause these days employers just cant be bothered with you. 'O' levels are nothing these days, and it wont be long till it'll be HIGHERS that are needed to get a job.
I left school without any 'O' levels because in the last year it was just a repeat of work you were doing and I just didn't think it was worthwhile staying on so I left, and that is why I started staying of school about the last 2 week as I was bored.
Don't get me wrong, it was my mum that got me my job as she is a Bookbinder by trade, but people might not be as lucky as I was and if

you ask me, I'd tell anybody else to stay on if
school could improve. But there are teachers
who tend to treat you like babies, and I think
that puts you off as wel, and then some of them
have time for others and not for you. Oh, it
makes me mad and if I had enough space, I'd
try and explain what teachers really are like and
how they teach some of their pupils.
Well thank you for sending this leaflet to me, I
am happy to oblige in filling this in. And I
hope it helps.
Girl, non-certificate Christmas leaver.
Apprentice bookbinder.

'Not very many teachers to teach us'
who suffered when teachers and their time were scarce?

I never liked the last year at school because
there was nothing to do and there was not very
many teachers to teach us. Most of the time we
were sitting for 1 hr 20 min doing nothing,
even when we had a teacher he or she just told
us to talk quitly among ourself or sit and draw
or whatever we wanted to do. I think that once
you were 16 and had a job to go to they should
have let you leave instead of keeping us back
another 4 or 5 months doing hardly anything. I
think that is why most of the people in the last
year played truant.
Girl, non-certificate. Unemployed.

I did not do my last year at school because
when we went in to school in the morning we
got our mark and we were sent home. So we
did not have to play truant in our last year we
just got sent home and that was that. Some
times my mother did not believe me and told
me to get back to school she thought, I was
playing truant but I wasint: she told us to go
and get a letter in my spare time after being
sent home I just played football.
PS You may not belive me but it is true.
Boy, non-certificate. Unemployed.

My last year at School was'nt much use as at
that time our school was on part time
Education and the school was short staffed we
more or less spent our time sitting our-selves, in
classrooms or in the Cloakroom. I did not like
that at all. The teachers done their best but that
was'nt much help we all wanted to leave and
look for work, some teachers even told us
although not in so many words that we were all

just wasting our time and their time. I think I
stopped going to school about October and
Nobody bothered at all, as soon as I got my
insurance number through I started to look for
work I got a job quite easy in a factory's day
nursery for mothers who had young children I
love my job and I would never ever dream of
leaving it now. But although I have not had
cause to look back my advise to all school
leavers is no matter what you want to be when
you leave school is to sit at least one "O" level.
Girl, non-certificate. Nursery assistant.

After my second year at school my class was
just thrown aside. As we did not qualifie for O
levels. So it was just a case of to hell with yous.
In my opinion this was to push the O'level
pupils on. And from 3rd year on it was part-
time education. We could sit in a arithmetic
class and end up writing a stupid essay because
the arithmetic teacher had to take an O level
class while we had a P.E. teacher. As for
guidance we sometimes got the odd film, but
usually ended up playing football or some other
game, because teacher was to busy. Our last
year and a half school was made up mostly of
metal work, woodwork, P.E. & Art. We would
go into school in the morning and get sent
home 2 hours later. Out of all the last year &
half you could have put what we where taught
into three months.
Boy, non-certificate. Venetian blind fitter.

My last year at school wasn't very good I was
on part time education two days a week I liked
woodwork and was hoping to be a joiner to
trade. The teachers couldn't help us very much
when I was just there two days a week. Im still
hoping to be an App. joiner Ive tried all around
but had no luck. So I will just have to bide in
the dairy to something better comes along.
*Boy, non-certificate. Cleans and fills milk
bottles.*

I found the teachers very understanding when I
was stuck with any problems. I quite enjoyed
school really except the last year where the
shortage of teachers meant having to sit in
classrooms for long periods at a time doing
nothing.
Girl, non-certificate. Unemployed.

Looking forward to leaving school because I did
not learn anything, and it was boring as were
always getting a day off here and there because
the more intelligent people were doing their O
levels. I did not like being pushed around as if I
was a nothing, I think I felt this way because I
could not sit O levels because my class was a
non certific class so the teachers had no time for

us. The teachers could have made my time more useful by paying a little more time to the girls and boys that couldn't sit O levels and were not so bright, and I think that when we got our lessons if we got something wrong in our work and if we tell them we do not know how to do something instead of explaining it properly to us they stand at their desks, and get very easily embarassed about that sort of thing, and by the time I try to get over my embarassment I am usually behing my work so I think I could be a lot better today if it wasnt for all that.

Girl, non-certificate. Unemployed.

My last year at school was more or less a waste of time for both me and the school. As my whole class was not taking "O" levels we were forgotten about a lot of the time or sent to the school "cafe" to sit and play cards and pass the time. During "O" level exams we were used to "police" the corridors or do jobs like that. As for education during my last year I would have been as well working. I think it would be a good thing if everybody in school had to take some "O" levels it would avoid a left-out feeling and a couldn't care less attitude of both teachers and pupils.

Boy, non-certificate. Apprentice farm worker.

The thing I liked about the last year at school was the way the teachers treated us. We were free to do anything we liked and most times did. But sometime we would be sitting around in the library or a classroom all day which made us very bored and this was the cause of some of the truances. The last six months at school we were never out of the gym room five aside, badmington, etc. which we all enjoyed.

Boy, non-certificate. Unemployed.

Well the only thing I liked on my last year at school was sewing and we did not get much of that becuse all we had to do was sit in coridas. If you are not inthe Upper class the teachers did not bother with you and I think that the ones that are not to good at there subjects they should get more help.

Girl, non-certificate. Unemployed.

I feel that the whole system of education in Scotland is a complete failure due to the lack of interest in pupils from members of staff. In my eyes they were only interested in the already bright pupils and were not prepared to really try and help the unfortunate less bright ones, instead they made massive classes of outcasts or as they would call them remedials. I spend my last term in a class without a teacher along with another twenty or so doing nothing at all. this

was because we weren't alougd to leave school in the summer, we had to stay on until Christmas becuase of ages, when we could have been out looking for jobs or even earning some money. It was clear that the school wasn't interested in us.

Boy, non-certificate. Studying O grades and Highers at FE college. Engineering tracer.

To me my last year at school was a waste of time. I was not sitting any O levels so the teachers never took much interest in me. I used to play truant frequently and was caught a number of times. I upset my parents and they could not understand why I played truant from school.

Girl, non-certificate. Works in a clothes factory.

What I liked about my school was they did not presure you into doing anything & what I did not like about school was you just went into classes & did nothing just tawk to the teacher our freinds that's why I played truant.

Boy, non-certificate. Apprentice, actual employment unknown.

My last year at school was a complete waste of time both for myself and the teaching staff. The teachers could not have helped, they were not greatly interested in someone who they knew would not be going on to higher level education.

Boy, non-certificate. Works in a shop owned by his family.

What I didn't like about my last year at school, was I thought it was quite boring in some subjects, and I think the teachers didn't really care for you any more, as you didn't have to study in your last year at school as there was no exams to sit; so they thought why should they waste there time on us anymore, because a lot of us just didn't listen to the teachers and that is why the teacher's usually lost interest in us. And I don't think the teachers could have made the time more useful for us, as they tried to do everything they could for us and I am grateful.

Girl, non-certificate. Assembly line worker.

In the last year of school some of the teachers new that I wasn't taking any O'levels so they didn't wast time pumping usless information into me. Having to go to school in my last year. It was a waste of time.

Boy, non-certificate. Fisherman.

I am now settled in my job and I know most of the people with whom I work, and I am learning more each day which makes me happy. I liked school in general. but I think 15 yrs of

age should be the leaving age. The last year
people like me learn nothing of any value. and
the teachers know this also.
  Girl, non-certificate. Clothes machinist.

The only time I enjoyed school was the first
three years of secondary because you were
learned different things each year and in second
year you go to pick your own subject, the last
year of secondary school was very booring
because you were being teached the same as the
year before and in most classes we were just
sitting listening to the radio or going to the
library. The thing I found difficult when I was
looking for work was that you did not have
enough qualifications or you were to young or
you did not have experience of any jobs that
were available. To help other young people who
will be leaving the school I think instead of just
sitting about their last year they could be
teaching them how to go about looking for a
job.
  Girl, non-certificate. Works in a factory.

I never really liked school, I don't no why but I
could not wait to leave for as long as I can
remember. I did not hate the teachers because
they had a job to do like any body else, I just
hated the place.
  *Boy. O grades, no A–C awards. Apprentice
  joiner.*

When I was at Shcool, I was always getting into
trouble, I was always carrying on with my
school friends and being cheeky to my
Teachers. However I found my teachers very
Patient and Symphatic towards me and my
schoolfriends, they seemed to know that we
were just passing the time in school, waiting for
a chance to leave and start work.
  Boy. O grades, no A–C awards. Warehouseman.

I hated school because our class was a low wone
so in the last year we did not get anything we
were alowed to gow out nater walks and get
loste untill the nexst day.
  Girl, non-certificate. Waitress.

Well what I think about school was I got on
with a few teachers but not a lot off my palls.
There was a few roughts in my class thats what
bothered me so that's what I thought. So there
you have my lot. Thank you for your letter.
  Boy. non-certificate. Unemployed.

CHAPTER THREE

'I DIDN'T GO TO SCHOOL
MY LAST YEAR'

Truancy

Yes I would like to tell you more about myself. I didn't go to school my last year, as I knew it would be a waste of time. I sell ginger to the public.

Boy, non-certificate, truanted 'weeks at a time'. Van boy for a soft drinks company.

As Table 4 in the Appendix makes quite plain, a majority of fourth year pupils in recent years have played truant. For example, among O grade leavers only three out of ten boys and four out of ten girls said they had 'never' truanted in their fourth year. A quarter had missed 'a lesson here and there', and a further quarter or more had missed a 'day here and there'. Similarly about half the pupils who went on to sit for Highers said they had missed a 'lesson' or a whole 'day' 'here and there' in their fourth year. These leavers had been asked 'Did you play truant in your fourth year at school?' and they could answer by indicating one of the phrases quoted above, or by choosing one of two more extreme categories, 'several days at a time' and 'weeks at a time', responses that we might, perhaps, regard as indications of 'serious' truancy. The data from the 1977 survey revealed for the first time two aspects of the phenomenon of serious truancy: its relatively even distribution over all the mainland Regions of Scotland, and the extent to which, in the fourth year, it was concentrated among pupils who were following non-certificate courses. A third of non-certificate boys and a quarter of non-certificate girls classed themselves as serious truants in that they had absented themselves from school for several days at a time, or for weeks at a time; and a follow-up interview study gave reason to believe most non-certificate pupils had described their own behaviour faithfully (Cope and Gray 1978). The proportion of serious truants among fourth year pupils who went on to Highers was trivial whilst among O grade leavers, it was about one in ten.

Why did such high proportions of non-certificate pupils absent themselves from school? Cope and Gray's conclusion after a systematic content-analysis of their reasons was as follows:

. . . we can legitimately infer that for non-Certificate pupils, the perceived irrelevance of much of their school work, the perceived inadequacy of the provision and their sense of being treated as relatively unimportant, all of which comes through so vividly in their volunteered statements, must at the very least have legitimised their truancy in their own eyes, may indeed have triggered it off, and certainly could not have countered other factors operating to induce them to absent themselves from school (*idem*).

The incidence of serious truancy, however, varied considerably between schools. In the quarter of schools where it occurred least frequently no more than six per cent of all pupils in any one school truanted seriously in fourth year; but in the quarter of schools where it occurred most frequently more than one in five pupils in each school said they had stayed off for days or weeks at a time (see Appendix, Table 7). The leavers' accounts of their truancy again and again came back to the quality of the non-certificate courses and of what went with them. They offer one insight into the phenomenon.

'No time for dunces'
rejection is mutual

The reason I never went to school the past year was because I was in a non sertificate class and the teachers had no time for dunces. we did not get any work of any kind every day at our different classes we just sat all day doing nothing and our exams last year were adding sums 'at our age'. It was terrible that was the only reason 4th year of 4D and 4C never went to school because I liked going to school up to then. Well thats all I have to say I would like to have said that to some of the teachers at _____ Academy.

Girl, non-certificate, truanted 'weeks at a time'. Works in a printing business.

My last year at school was not very good because they had no time for us as they were more interested in Pupill's who were takeing O-levels they had no dirffent corese for us to do So I just played truent, I am now waiting to join the army.

Boy, non-certificate, truanted 'weeks at a time'.

I diden't attend school reguarly because in my last year the school dident give us any thing of intrest, I was in one of the lower classes and we dident get O level work. I myself think that all classes should be made the same because if you are in the lower clases you lose all intrest in school. I think that that when someone like myself leaves school it is hard to find a job because every where you go they want experiance. Every young person looking for work after leaving school should be given the same chance as anyone else whether they have O grades or not.

Girl, non-certificate, truanted 'weeks at a time'. Waitress.

Well about my last year at school it was virtually a waste of time going because there was not all that many members in the class 8 people to be precise. Very often a few members would not turn up and the teachers did not think it worth while teaching the class. I think it would have been much better if we had not been branded as being thick and not worth bothering about. The lessons we did get were often dull and boring but the subjects that we liked such as technical work and physical education seemed to be the lessons that we got the least of. I think school would have been much better if the teachers had tried to communicate with the pupils and asked them

what subjects would be most useful to them and also most interesting.

Boy, non-certificate, truanted 'a day here and there'. Panel beater.

Well to tell you the truth about the last year at school I hated the whole lot of it because every class we went into the majority of the teachers would be their about 5–10 minutes then go off and leave us until about 5 minutes before our two periods were up. And it was very boring and thats why in the last year I and my friend palyed truant. The teachers could have made it more useful if they were in the class teaching us instead of leaving us an exercise to do which never got done because they never asked for it when they came back.

Girl, non-certificate, truanted 'several days at a time'. Shop assistant.

I think the last year at school was not of any use because the teachers didn't bother about you because you were leaving school so I played truant. I didn't like periods all broke up for different subjects. I think I would have been better off leaving school at 15. I now have a job and I work for a good firm. It only took me 1 week to get a job and I was hardly ever at school I never realy was off at my primary school it was worth going too much better than secondary any day the teachers took notice of you there.

Girl, non-certificate, truanted 'several days at a time'. Cloth machinist.

I didn't go to school much my last year I think it was because of the teachers as they didn't have time for people like me.

Girl, non-certificate, truanted 'weeks at a time'. Unemployed.

When I went to school the reason I played truant so much was because I hated the teachers, for the simple reason that I wasn't to bright at school, and if I didn't catch something the teacher said, or couldn't do something right, I was scared to ask the teacher, because eight out of ten would just tell me I should have been listning or to just get a copy off of a freind, so when it came to exams I just didn't have a clue what to do. I feel that if the teacher tried to help me more I would have got on alot better at school, also if the teachers try to help you with personal problems it would also be alot easier. What I found most difficult trying to find a job was that I had no qualifications. I think that what someone wants to do for a career Every-thing sould be done to help him or her. That's the only way realy that anyone will get some satisfaction out of life. I mean I asked the career

oficer for something to do in the line of a beautician and she got me a job in a shop. So realy what would be best is to get them the O' levels then it wont be so hard. Thanking you.
Girl. O grades, no A–C awards. Truanted 'weeks at a time'. Shop assistant.

If given the chance I would have left school as earlier than possible because our last year was a waste of time, we just went to our subjects and were told by teachers, 'Do something to ocupie yourself,' consisting of talking, laughing around and often playing cards, most of the class were fed-up of this going on for months so many people thought it a better idea to dodge a few periods, so you can't blame them things were that boring, pupils just got out of the road of them.
Boy, non-certificate, truanted 'a lesson here and there'. Unemployed.

I hated my last year at school the teachers didint give *that* for you. But I very rarely went to school in my last year because of this.
Boy, non-certificate, truanted 'weeks at a time'. Stock clerk.

School was alright in my last year but I very seldom went as I found not very much interest was put into it and it was a bit of a waist of time in most classes I sat and done nothing and after sitting doing nothing it takes away your concentration for your next class where work had to be done.
Girl. O grades, no A–C awards. Truanted 'several days at a time'. On a work experience scheme as a shop assistant.

'I did not like my teacher'
specific problems

I liked most of the teacher's, and some of the subjects. I did not like my Geography class or teacher that was mostly why I was alway's playing truant, it was always that period, because he was far too strict, and I did not have enough time to Learn it.
Girl, non-certificate. Lace worker.

In my final years I was put into a class to study social sciance. this subject was to be no use in my choosen carrer, the carrer officer should have helped me in the selection of O leavel subjects which would be pertinent in gaining employment. In trying to change my classes to get further on in Maths department was not a

lot of help, that pupils who wanted to learn soon gave up trying, and as a consequences this led to truance and missing classes I to my own discredit was guilty of this offence myself.
Boy. O grades, no A–C awards. Truanted a lesson 'here and there'. Unemployed.

I was stupid in school i was not interested. my maths teacher was to bisy to do anything with my class in English i always played truant.
Girl, non-certificate, truanted a lesson 'here and there'. Employment unknown.

I wrote I played truant several day's at a time, in fact we done in for weeks but maybe every afternoon of the day and sometimes full days. I don't think I got a fair chance at one subject in particular accounts. he was a nasty old bachelor and he got on at me and my friends and that is why I played truant so much. He also had us for typing and that is why I didn't get my 'O' level. He said to us before we left school if you come back here next year you'll have to beg on your knee's if you want into my class.
Girl. O grades, no A–C awards. Truanted 'several days at a time'. Unemployed.

The advice I would give to someone still at school is not to truant unless it is a subject that he/she really hated and did not sit an O-level in (eg. I used to truant when I had religious education I hated the subject I found it boring and a waste of time). I think that there should be a chance a school to sit an exam in P.E. as a lot of people I know would have sat this exam me encluded. I also feel that if you don't think a subject is helping you (eg. R.E.) you should be aloud to do some other subject instead. I know if that had been possible I would not have played truant on the day I got Religious Ed and I would not have been put on a truant slip and hunted every morning by the deputy headmaster.
Girl. O grades, no A–C awards. Truanted 'a lesson here and there'. Bottling operator.

All I can say a bout my self if I am shy and nervous and do my fare share of work and I never go out at night. I was hardly ever at school the last year cause I never liked it as I never had anybody to go about with and when I had to answer a question my face went all red because the people in my class started to look at me and I would get all mixed up and make a fool of myself and the teacher would make it worse for me as they made me sit at the front of the class and I was scared to answer in case I was wrong and they would all laugh at me. I don't really know if he could have made the time more useful. I'm sure it was up to myself to make the time more useful.

Girl, non-certificate, truanted 'weeks at a time'. Working in a baking factory.

'The teachers never asked why'
did school care?

The last year at school was the one I will remember most as it was about the only year at school I enjoyed. But in the last six months of school I started playing truant (this because of personal reasings). I would stay off a few days come back take my punishment and then the next week I would stay off again. The teachers never asked why, or asked if you were having problems. They would just belt you and that was that. Thats whats wrong with them they dont understand young people and how our minds works. They gave me a lot of trouble.

Boy, non-certificate, truanted 'weeks at a time'. In a manual job.

I felt that in the last year at school the teachers did not bother about you if you were not taking o levels eg. (they know we played truant and never sayed anything to us about it).

Girl, non-certificate, truanted 'a lesson here and there'. Unemployed.

The last year at school was terrible. We would go into a class and the teachers might not even come in so we were left there by ourselves. Nothing to do. Sometimes the teachers would come in and say I have some correcting to do, Well that wasn't teaching us anything. It was right boring. There was hardly anybody there as the year went on more and more people would stay of they didnt bother getting us back again you could walk pass a teacher in the street and say 'hello' they would just return the remark and just walk past. The best thing I liked about the last year at school was when it was finished. They could have made the time more useful by teaching us the subject we were in the class for, I have been partly looking for a job since I left school and going back and forward to the hospital. I would like to look after children be a nannie or something like that.

Girl, non-certificate, truanted 'weeks at a time'. Unemployed.

Well for the class I was in at my last year at school was boring. It was a class that they didn't bother with. I don't think they would

have bothered if you were off or not. I didn't waste the bus fare going much as I thought it was a bore. When I left school I didn't have a job as I didnt look for one. But a 3 month later I got a job in a local factory in _____ and then when I started work I just said 'I wish I could go back to school and do all the days I was off'. As I hated it. But know I work in a place with a lot of people my age, and it is a great laugh.

Girl, non-certificate. Working in a shoe factory.

I quite liked School, But my last two years I got nothing to do, just the same things I felt it was the waste of time, while I was waiting on a Job. I helped my Mother in the House so I think I'm good at Domestic Work as well. I think anyone who is ready to leave School shoud be able to stay off and look for work with out the School Officer being sent to the house and get taken to the Panel thats what happen to me I feel I have learned quite a lot after I left School. I can look after myself earn money and watch how I spend it I help my Mother weekdays and go out at Week ends with my Pals. I hope I have helped you by answering the questions. So its alright if anyone is going to work in an office to take any o levels , or stay on.

Girl, non-certificate, truanted 'weeks at a time'. Works in a textile mill.

I quite liked school, but the last few months were really boring. There were alot of free periods etc. That is why most of the pupils intending to leave played truant. One time, school even threatened truants with court action against the parents. It shouldn't be compulsory to go to school the last few months. I really like my job. It is really interesting I think pupils intent on leaving should have the last months of school more interesting and have job exsperience.

Boy. O grades, no A–C awards. Truanted 'weeks at a time'. Apprentice mechanic.

'I went fishing'
what truants did with their time

I do not like fighting and I like listening to records I liked School a little bit. when I doged school I did not do what the rest of them do I went fishing as it is my best past time and I also done some sports.

Boy, non-certificate, truanted 'a lesson here and there'. Steel worker.

The only time that I liked in school is the times that I could play truant. Because then I could go to the local library and study at my leisure. Whereas in school the teachers are hanging over you all the time making pupils nervous. Or they would stand there talking on and on about something that even themselves dont know about.
(I think that self teaching myself was better than the teachers teaching me).

Boy, non-certificate, truanted 'weeks at a time'. Unemployed since he left school.

I don't think my last year at school was much good, because in most classes we did not get any work to do, it was very boring I used to play truant a lot because my time was more useful at home. I like my job but sewing we got at school wasnt a great help to me. I was fortunate enough to be able to pick it up easy. My job is very interesting you dont do the same things every day there is a wide variety.

Girl, non-certificate, truanted 'several days at a time'. Seamstress in a furniture business.

'But now I regreat it'
regrets

To tell you the truth I hated my school. Because I thought it was a complet waste of time as I did not learn much as that was my own fault for truanting. But now I regreat it and asamed of my self. And there was one thing I would have loved to have done was to pass my O level's.

Girl, non-certificate, truanted 'weeks at a time'. Shop assistant.

I thought my schooling years were terrible, I was always behind in my work mainly because of Trauncy. I tried hard at School, In my last two years, studied for five o' levels, but I left before I could take them. If I had worked harder at school instead of playing truant, which I regret now, I think I would have made a better career for myself. But things have worked out fine now. I think young people nowadays should be Presuaded that hard work at school and good attendance work out better for them in later years. I hope I have helped with your survey Yours truly

Boy, non-certificate, truanted 'several days at a time'. Labourer.

I quite enjoyed school even though I did not go, but now I wish that I had as I feel that I have missed most of my education which I now regret.

Girl, non-certificate, truanted 'weeks at a time'. On a work experience scheme as a secretary.

The last year at school they just dump you with any subject some of them were boaring it was just an excuse to keep you in school. That's how I played truant so often if they give you subjects that you like maybe they would be a lot of pupil would stay on to the end of term.

Boy, non-certificate. Unemployed.

'I wanted out anyway'
no regrets

I am the kind of person who liked to speak her mind. As you have found out by the answers to the Questions I didn't really like school, in fact I hated it, that's why I played truant or as we would say 'dogged it'. The teachers should give kids a better chance and once the reach there last year treat them like an adult. Oh yes! they tell you that you are growing up to be a fine young Lady/Gentlemen, but they never treat you like one. Thats why I have had six jobs because when somebody stands on my toes they better watch out as I tell them what I think about them. But don't get me wrong I am not a hard woman although I sound to you as if I am. I was the first one in my school to stand up to the teachers and the head master so they didn't like it and they expelled me. My parents fought for me but I told them to forget it because I wanted out anyway. Maybe I have the wrong attitude but there you have me.

Girl, non-certificate, truanted 'days at a time'. Unemployed.

I did not like school because the teacher's were very bossey. But I like working because I can look forward to a wage at the end of the week. At work you can talk and have a laugh and still do your own number but at school you talk and get the belt I make my own wages and think it is much better. I was never at school but I am always at my work I am never off I hate being off my work it is so interesting but school is boring.

Girl, non-certificate, truanted 'weeks at a time'. She describes her job as 'under-presser. Press the tip's and seam's of ties'.

'The only thing in my point of view to help pupils now is . . .'
suggestions for change

Well I enjoyed school when I went but I did not got very often in my last year and that was only because I had a job cleaning cars in the same place as I am in now I started working in this showroom when I was 14 at the weekends then after 3 months I started to work full time instead of going to school I would go to work and my parents did not aprove when they found out 6 months later when my mother took a day of work and had the attendance officer. I also went to the children's panel for not attending school. Well after that I went to school and then I just wasn't intrested in school work it was so silly having to go to school when I could be working so I was determind not to go and then the time came after I left the work to go back to school as I was forced to go I just went to keep my parents happy. But I was just not interested in school. It was terrible being forced to go to school when I didn't want to I was also threatened to be put in a home if I didn't attend. But as much as I hated school I love working ther is AIM in working it is so worth while apart from the money you have a Carrer and it is not as if you are being treated as a child. When you are ADULT But teachers just dont understand. When I was ask why I did not have any interest in school by my housemaster, I explained about my job I was told I was just being silly and I was told then that I was to study my subjects as he new that I could do them. But it was not enough for me as I began then to hate the teachers who told me this they all seemed to say I had plenty of time to work when I left school. But now I am just glad that I did not listen to them. Now, well I just took my chance and I know I made it as I see my freinds that stayed on get there O levels and now have to sign the 'DOLE'. But now I feel sorry for the people in school the only thing in my point of view to help pupils now is the teachers listen to the children's views' and realise how STRONG the pupils feel and not tell the children they are being SILLY. Because it could have had me on the DOLE as well if I had listened. By saying this I dont mean the pupil to be just stubern but to listen and think very carefully before commitment. But this all lies inbetween both the pupils' and teachers ALSO PARENTS to help and understand I also realise that the teachers have a ruff time to look after the pupils and teache them I also

wish the teachers the best of luck they need it. As I think this is a very good idea to give pupils this form I also hope this help's pupils and also teachers as teachers need as much help as pupils and the teachers have a lot to contend with.

Girl, non-certificate, truanted 'a day here and there'. Works in a showroom.

Dear Sir,
I was NEVER at school when I was in 2nd and 3rd year. When I went back to school they put me in a special class of dogers. It was something they were trying out. It was to help us to stop playing truant. We went to the Baths, a run in the Teachers car, we made tablet and sell it to School. The teacher let us cut out page THREE in the Daily Record. and put it up on the classroom wall. When we left the school they stop the class. But to me they should have KEPT IT OPEN it would have done a lot for young people. Yours.

Boy, non-certificate, truanted 'several days at a time'. Labourer.

Please read this Don't ignore it that's what you probably would have done.
What I liked about my last year at school was I got doing what I wanted to do which was very wrong the teachers should have been more striked with their orders instead they were soft they even let some of the boys swear at them and some of the teachers would just laugh which made us laugh to what has happened to tough *BOYS* and *GIRLS* is not only their fault it is the parents and the teachers and other important people who do this. Yes I really enjoyed my last year at school thats why I played truant for weeks. No I really detested every single year either you get a soft teacher or you get a striked teacher the soft ones didn't bother and to much a striked teacher made you scared you know to be a teacher you need to know more than English, maths, Geography, History etc. You need to learn to get through to a class full of kids and grown ups just like real parents need to do the same. *PATCIENCE* would be a *good thing for them.*

Girl, non-certificate, truanted 'weeks at a time'. Unemployed.

CHAPTER FOUR

'TOO GOOD WITH THE BELT'

Corporal punishment and discipline

I didn't like the teachers very much in my opinion they were too good with the belt. The teachers could have been more useful if they would have let you have your say in matters. They treated you like first year pupils. My last year at school was only a big laugh and to see your friends. On my last 2 years at school I was in part time education.

Girl, non-certificate, belted 'often'. Unemployed.

'The tension Showed, on the teacher's face, when They Couldn't get Something Through to you,' wrote one non-certificate girl who left school to become unemployed. She continued, 'because of vast overcrowding She Couldn't Control the lot of us . . .'. If truancy can partly be understood as one response to the felt inadequacy of school provision and of relationships with teachers, so also can indiscipline. A leather belt or strap applied to the open palm of the hand has been a widely accepted form of corporal punishment in Scotland although in recent years its effectiveness, morality and even legality have been hotly debated mostly, it must be said, against a background of public ignorance as to the manner, frequency and occasions of its use. A code of practice drawn up by officials of the Scottish Education Department and by educationists who were mainly members of the larger teacher unions in Scotland recommended that the belt should only be used 'as a last resort, and should be directed to punishment of the wrong-doer and to securing the conditions necessary for order in the school and for work in the classroom' (SED 1968). Against this recommendation we may set actual practice as described by pupils and leavers themselves.

In something like ten per cent of schools, corporal punishment seems to have been rarely used in that none of the leavers sampled from these schools said they had been physically punished either 'quite often' or 'often' during their secondary school years (Appendix, Table 7). In a further 15 per cent of schools less than ten per cent of all the leavers sampled from each school said they had experienced frequent corporal punishment, so defined. At the other extreme, in the 25 per cent of schools where frequent corporal punishment was most common, more than a quarter of all the leavers from each school said they had been punished in this way 'quite often' or 'often'. At the extreme of this group of schools were some ten per cent of all schools in each of which at least 36 per cent of all their leavers said they had been physically punished 'quite often' or 'often'.

Looking at pupils rather than schools, as we may in Table 5 of the Appendix, striking differences, so to speak, are apparent between the experience of Highers, O grade and non-certificate boys and girls. Among girls the percentages who said they had been physically punished 'quite often' or 'often' at secondary school were, respectively, 2, 14 and 26 per cent. (The code of practice had required that, '. . . only in exceptional circumstances should . . . girls be strapped at all'.) Among boys they were 23, 50 and 60 per cent. Indeed, one non-certificate girl in ten (10 per cent), and one non-certificate boy in four (27 per cent) answered in terms of the 'often' category. Whilst the logical problems of comparing and quantifying different experiences ultimately precludes a definitive measurement of the frequency of corporal punishment, whether based on the accounts of leavers or on those of teachers, advisers or Inspectors, it nevertheless seems that the last resort is quite often reached in the school life of at least a large minority of non-certificate pupils and in a large minority of schools.

The leavers' accounts of 'strap happy' teachers in the opening section are largely dominated by the experience of conflict and aggression, some leavers making it plain that they '. . . went to school to cause trouble . . .', others complaining that some teachers behaved arbitrarily and that '. . . there should be notices on boards Telling pupils what teachers can tell you to do and can't'.

For some leavers by this stage, '. . . School was a place where you could see all your friends, and have a laugh. Some of the teachers were a good laugh and could take a Joke but there were a few teachers who treated you like dirt.' Many of the leavers, indeed, discussed belting in the context of judgements that discriminated between different teachers and between good and bad experiences at school. This indicates that, whilst such leavers may have felt strongly about corporal punishment, the strength of their feelings on this issue had not entirely swamped their capacity to judge other aspects of their schooling. Comments of this type have been collected mainly in the section, 'The thing I liked about my school . . . but'. Amongst other things they give one confidence that, whilst resentment and bravado may have played some part in influencing responses to the fixed-alternative question on corporal punishment, such influence as they had has not markedly affected the distribution of responses.

Some leavers were at pains to emphasise 'I know you need some rules'. On occasion, as we have already seen, this may have been for their own protection: '. . . I got on with a few teachers but not a lot off my palls. There was a few roughts in my class thats what bothered me so that's what I thought. So there you have my lot'. Rules relating to personal habits and manners (dress, chewing gum and smoking) seemed particularly irksome, though not always in the context of belting. 'Being treated like a kid' is a phrase that summarises much of the non-certificate pupils' hostility to this aspect of the school regime.

Striking a balance between order and freedom and negotiating what it is to be adult would, nevertheless, appear to pose great difficulties. In one leaver's eyes, teachers could not win: 'Some are too hard and some too soft'. Another leaver was 'on the receiving end of endless torment' from her class and asked for 'less sympathy and more action'. But, behind a third account one detects determined efforts by teachers to accommodate a disruptive pupil: 'I liked my school because of the warm friendly atmosphere. Most of the teachers are kind and understanding even although I was difficult and cheeky at school. I was supposed to take seven 'O' levels at school but I had no interest in any of them so I just mucked about and disrupted the whole class'. Some leavers thought they were being treated as adults when they were given less work to do in their final year; others thought they were being disregarded when teachers allowed them to do what they wanted.

'What would stop the children running riot and doing anything they want' was the somewhat plaintive question of a leaver who became a tractor driver. He could see no alternative to the belt 'because teachers would have no power across children'. He asked, 'Please let me know what would stop them doing this'. In fact his fellow leavers had few alternatives to suggest to the sanction of belting. It was rare also for suggestions to be made for the wider adoption of examples of good practice that pupils had witnessed. The few that were mentioned, however, carry a certain plausibility if only because they return to a by now familiar theme: 'The teachers at the school I went to just havent got any interest in these pupils. If the teachers gave us more hard work and had helped us with it I think girls and boys like us would stick in and get all there O levels and such things. I really enjoyed my last year at school because teachers could trust us and make us feel grown up and we never needed any of her help. She just stood and watched us if we made a mistake she would correct us not just jump up and wack us. I think that belting a pupil is no use. It just brings the worst out on them. If they do anything stupid they should be corrected and not belted . . .'. Contrast this with the experience of the girl with which this introduction opened: 'I would have liked the teacher to have spent a little more time with me, but due to the overcrowded classes, They didn't have enough time, The tension Showed on the teacher's face . . .'

'Strap happy'
views on corporal punishment

My opinion is that my last year at school was wasted because the teachers had no time for any pupils unless they were brainy. Some of the teachers were strap happy.

Boy, non-certificate, belted 'often'. Labourer

The teachers at school used to annoy me when they used to treat us as children and they all thought they were masters or something with their straps using them to try and frighten you espesialy the first year pupils, but it didnt work with us and this used to make them mad. Then some of them would try to man handle you and this wasn't on so when you told them to leave off, you were the bad one and taken to the rector and he was told that you were just a little holagin.

Boy, non-certificate, belted 'often'. Fisherman.

I didn't like anything about my school! What I didn't like was the teachers attitude towards pupils who were not very bright! Some teachers tryed to stamp their authority on pupils by threatning them with the belt!

Boy. O grades, no A–C awards. Apprentice electrician.*

The only thing I liked about school was P.E. Because the teacher could talk to you as if he was your pal and he had a good sense of humour.
I did'nt like school because the teachers told each other about you and harass you and wait for you to step out of Place and that was their excuse to belt you.

Boy, non-certificate, belted 'often'. Unemployed

School was a waste of time for me I never learnt much. People who are not taken 'O' grades should get periods for guidance in getting jobs learning how to write to firms and things like that. Teachers shouldn't give you the belt for half the thing they give you it for. There should be notices on boards Telling pupils what teachers can tell you to do and can't. And what they can give you the belt if you don't do your homework which you are not allowed to.

Boy, non-certificate, belted 'often'. On a work experience scheme.

Ive got on quite well since I left school because I was one of the lucky one's who got a job waiting for me. I really quite like my job now and get on well with everyone, and I feel myself, that I have grown up a lot since I left school. Going back to school ag n. What I didn't like at school is taking a subject that I hated, and knew I would never make anything of it, such as maths which I quite liked at first, but the teacher never explained the questions we got and therefore at the end of the lesson I hardly done any so I got the belt. What I did like at school was cookery probably because we got a step by step lesson on that and therefore I could do it and enjoy doing it.

Girl, non-certificate. Sewing machinist.

The things I liked about Schools was that you change teacher every 35 minuites, which meant you did not get board. Also the subjects that I took when I was at school were very interesting. The things I didint like about School was that you got treated like a young school child. Some teachers where letting there Position go to there heads and giving you the *strap*.

Boy, non-certificate, belted 'quite often'. Apprentice panel beater.

The only thing I liked about school was subjects like Art, Woodwork or Phyisical education, because In my forth year at school I lost Interest In other subjects, well I liked English and I did'nt liked being knocked around by teachers or getting the belt, or homework.

Boy, non-certificate, belted 'quite often'. Working in a tool factory.

There was only a few things I liked about School. The School was a place where you could see all your friends, and have a laugh. Some of the teachers were a good laugh and could take a Joke but there were a few teachers who treated you like Dirt. There were the ones who thought they were Something great and realy Put you off School the way they ordered you about and belted you for just making Coments.

Boy, non-certificate. Apprentice plasterer.

I was never happy in school since the day I started, secondary school was the worsed because of the way the teachers acted towards you. To them you were shit, and they pushed you around a lot. When I got the belt it did not cure me it made me want to get own back on them. Even now I want to go back and punch

* The question on corporal punishment was asked in only some of the versions of the questionnaires. Where details of punishment are omitted, the respondent had received a questionnaire version that did not ask about corporal punishment.

the bastards one on the mouth. As for looking for a job I cant thank the careers ofice enough for helping me.

Boy, non-certificate, belted 'often'. Armature winder.

I didn't like school because some of the teachers were to bossie. Take my P.E. teacher he thot he was the head Master. IF things was not going his way he would BELT the first Boy that spoke and if thay refused thay would get exspelled so we had to take the BELT.

Boy, non-certificate: Unemployed.

I think teachers try to Brain wash you putting things into your head for eg I spoken to people from Russia they say it's a good place but teachers say its bad and treats people rotten and I think teachers think there big heroes giving inocent kids the belt too look big when he can just as well give them a man to man talk.

Boy. O grades, no A–C awards. Belted 'often'. Catering trainee.

For a start I did'nt learn much my last year as I did 4 yearth twice and could not learn much, teachers did'nt help much. The belt was most unfair, we got it for not having a pen or pencil, being late, not doing homework or if someone done something wrong and was not found out we all got it.

Boy, non-certificate, belted 'once or twice'. Van boy.

In school I would like a less formal atmosphere in class where the pupil can talk on a personal basis with the teacher.

Also in school some teachers tend to slag a lot and expect to be treated as high and mighty and not take anything back in reply, but when there is a reply, the belt was often produced, I think these teachers are just childish and think they are the king of the castle.

Boy, non-certificate. Apprentice draughtsman.

I didn't like anything about my last year at school. I didn't like the teachers, you were belted for the least thing, we were getting work that we got in first year.

Boy, non-certificate, belted 'quite often'. Unemployed.

I liked school but becuse I always got into trouble the teachers never liked me. In my class at school the boy's liked a good laugh now and then the rector never liked me becused I always smirked when he spoke to me. At one time I got suspended I me ant four other boys caused a barney for 3 days the one teacher I never liked was the French teacher he hit me across

the face with a belt. There are a lot of things I could tell you but there is not any room.

Boy, non-certificate. Employment unknown.

I would just like to mention that I am a stupid little turd.

I used to be good at school till I went into third year. I was fourth in my class in first year, and first in second. I don't know what happened maybe the work was harder but my work got worse and worse. The work was harder of course but I just never had the brains to cope. I hated school just because I'm lazy. But teachers, I hated most of them, one told my best mates mum that I was holding him back and you can guess what happened the next time I went to his house. Some teachers are real evil and they never seem to be wrong? The belt I'm not against its needed to keep fools like me in their place. But I am against is the way if you do something bad big giant woodwork teachers really lay it on but when you come up against a female there's no way she will be able to hurt you as much as they evil things did. And this is for the same offence. They let their tempers run riot and leave your hands red raw.

The school I was at is one of the toughest in _____and the teachers are too soft. You found it hard to study when there was a load of evil lads around. Depending on the the class, some you could work in (although I always had a laugh anywhere) some you couldn't (I never had laugh in them). The teacher was so soft in my arithmetic class every week was games. But you couldn't ask for a move because if the rest of the class found out you were for it. Nearly every class I went to the teachers were always telling me I was imature and they were damn right. But I wish now they had kept me in line when I think about it, nearly everything I've written here is about me I'm sorry for that.

Boy. O grades, no A–C awards. Clerk.

The thing I liked was modern studies. Because we did what we wanted but I did not like the teacher so we picked on him then I got expelled for fighting with him and refusing the belt. My own fult. Thasts why me and my mates went to school to cause trouble cos we did not like teachers. They teachers could of treated us like peapole instead of animals. I have called all sorts of names by the teachers included a Bastard. I have looked for jobs but it's nae use they all say that theres nae jobs even the broo. P.S. I think theres to meny young teachers in school most look only 2 year older then me when I was at school and they all say the same things, and the belt just causes more trouble.

Boy, non-certificate, belted 'often'. Unemployed.

'The thing I liked about my school . . . but . . .'
some leavers who enjoyed school also commented on corporal punishment

The thing I liked about my school was the open plan design, friendliness of most of the teachers and extra curriculum activities. I did not like some of the school rules e.g. uniform, also I did not like the strap, it is a barbaric form of punishment.
Boy, non-certificate, belted 'quite often'.
Labourer at a car wash.

History was my best subject at school I liked the way the school was run, and that you had a choice of subjects. I also liked school dinners. The thing I disliked about school was that they treated you to much like a child. Also the strap, I disliked it the most.
Girl, non-certificate, belted 'once or twice'.
Textile machinist.

What I liked about school was the many friend's I made and the few teachers I liked were the one's that joked with us. I feel that if the teachers act like kids instead of showing their authority then the class and the teachers would get on better. What I did not like about school was belt happy teachers who if they did not like a person they picked on him. Just because you are a PUNK Rocker or a hippy doesn't mean you love the belt or being bullied. The school I attended wasn't as strict as others which you have to do this, watch this. I think you should be free to do or don't, wear what you want, and look away if you want because if you dont want to learn, Why should you and getting the belt for disobaying an order teaches you nothing and you just become more dissobediant.
Boy, non-certificate, belted 'quite often'.
Works in a slaughter house.

The most thing that I liked about school was that how clean the teachers kept the school. The thing I didn't like about the school was the way the teachers treated you as if you were some kid in _____ and they all liked given the belt.
Boy, non-certificate, belted 'once or twice'.
Unemployed.

I liked school and I wish I was still there because we used to have a great time, and I miss all my PALS because we used to have a great laugh. I didn't like school some days because of the Teachers They always said that we were smoking when we wer'nt but we still got the belt. I find it hard to get on with some of the older men I don't know why but I don't seen to get on with them because they are always telling you what to do and they order you about. just because they no a bit than me.
Boy, non-certificate, belted 'quite often'.
Engineering worker.

School was all right the only thing I did not like about school was the prefects they were a load of Bullies and licked to show off their authorities and if you hit them back you got lines or the strap and the teacher would always side with the prefect. In my High school some of the teachers really understood what a 15-16 year old likes doing and they would give you more of that work, mixed in with the stuff you did not like personally I liked my HIGH SCHOOL.
Boy, non-certificate. Bricklayer's labourer.

I liked P.E. at school I did not like school because you get the belt like say you got caught smoking and you mother and father let you smoke well they would still give you the belt but if your mother and father lets you smoke they should not belt you.
Boy. O grades, no A–C awards. Apprentice painter.

I was treated well at my school but I got in with the wrong people and was all way in trouble. In my last year at school I was all way told I had brains but just would not use them. With the teachers knowing what I was like any time there was trouble and I was around they would always look at me and try to blame me. Some of the teachers I liked and always tried to keep me out of trouble but I just would not listen. As far the belt being abolished I think they have alot of power behind them with it. Whenever I was to get the belt I always refused because some teachers cut your wrists with it and never hit you write on the palm.
Boy. O grades, no A–C awards. Belted 'quite often'. Works in a garage parts department.

'I know you need some rules'

opposition to corporal punishment as a sanction

School was alright at times but most of the time is was boaring. Most of the teachers was helpful but some if you did not come up to their standers they did not bother with you.
There is too many rules at schools I know you need some rules to keep people in line. Some teachers treat you like wee kids, write in blue pen, cover your jotter, draw a margine, take your coats off & were is your uniform or empty your mouth.

Girl. O grades, no A–C awards. Unemployed.

The school was fair. They knew what you didnt like and what you like. The thing I didnt like was the Rules. You couldnt wear denims, couldnt stay in the building when its dry, if you were standing in the corridor you would get checked or maybe essay or 100 lines to do.

Girl, non-certificate. Shop assistant.

I liked my School because it was friendly, and the headmaster took an interest in what everybody was doing, if you had a problem he was always ready to help. What I did not like about my School was Late Slips, if you were late for School you got one of these if you had three you were send too the head teacher you got a choice of writing out the School rules or the belt (which was quite fair but you would still get one if you were 10 seconds late). I dont think teachers should be allowed to give the pupils the belt I think it is daft.

Girl, non-certificate. Clothes machinist.

In my last year at school teachers started to treat you a little better and gave you more privilleges, and they would talk to you more. I didn't like the way they treated us like kids trying to get us to line up and call them Sir when you wanted to say anything. There were teachers much smaller than us and because he was in charge of the class he would want to bully us and belt us all the time and I don't think they should need to belt someone at the age of 16.

Boy, non-certificate. Apprentice upholsterer.

The main thing I liked about school was being able to choose some of my own subjects and being able to communicate quite easily with some of the teachers. I did not like some of

their rules EG; (You were not allowed to smoke) this I think is stupid because it's your own life thats at risk no one elsies and the biggest majority have their parents consent and smoke in front of them.

Boy, non-certificate. Apprentice painter and decorator.

I liked the teachrs, I got on with all of them. I liked the subjects that I had although they were hard. I didn't like some of the rules they had in school, I didn't like getting the belt. I loved it at the end of terms when we had our Discos.

Girl, non-certificate, belted 'once or twice'. Bingo caller.

The Thing the I did not like about my school or any schools is that there are people who try and people who don't care. And the teachers get so feed up of the boys who don't care. And then stop teaching the whole class. And therefore the people who want to lisining does'nt get a chance to.
I know this because a group of boys, who come in my work were good. And we would never have to watch them. And a couple of month again there was a couple of hard boys started to come in. My brother told me that every boy does what ever that want to and that is smoke and steal. Why does the schools not have some sort of private place where they could go and talk to a teacher of someone about being bulled. They would hardly go home and tell there mums that the boys in my class all smoke, and if I don't I get battered. I think schools should be forlearning good things and not bad.
I think myself that some teachers are scared of them. So if they say no homework that is how it will be. I think schools are very strict when you are in first or second year and then after that things like uniform, smoking and being cheaky to the teacher just does not matter so much. How can the teachers expect to keep a class in order, how.
I dont thing that the punishment that a boy gets is not enough. I remember in my class boys would have compitions who cauld get belted the most within a week. I think it would help if there was more time spent before they leave school, to have more time Finding out more jobs which would be suited for them.
I think it would help the teaches to have seperate boys and girls classes. That is if the boys and girls dont lissen. There cauld be more lectures on what happens when going into a now job.
When I left school The only thing that I now about tax or vat was what my dad told me. You sould be helped to find a job of your choice in early years at school, there is always a lot of

changing of subjects. You always hear people saying that they sat the wrong subject at school. I think it is the teachers folt.

Now they are to interested in do we or dont we get a day off with the teacher stricts. [strikes?]

Girl, non-certificate, 'never' belted. Shop assistant.

'Some are too hard and some are too soft'
striking a balance

I would blame a Teacher for pupils playing Truant. Some are too hard and some too soft. I am now applying for a job as an apprentice mining engineer. A miners job isn't bad but I would like to better my self in the coal mining industry. If I had another chance I would have stayed on at school.

Boy, non-certificate. Unemployed.

I liked the school I was at, but some of the teachers were far, far too soft. The pupils are there to learn not to fling Rubbers, at the teacher to to walk out when the feel like it, or to tell the teacher what to do and sware at them and get off with it. Now what I liked about my school, Some teachers were stricked but good like _____ P.E. instructor great teacher, _____ was very good aswel, _____ good teacher as well and one or two others not many but some .

Boy, non-certificate, belted 'once or twice'. Shop assistant.

I would say that my last two years at school were a waste of time. I hated school and think that something should be done to protest the weaker members of the school from persication and bullying. The teachers did nothing to help one from being at the recieving end of endless torment, this affected my work and landed me incapable of sitting any O grades. So lets see less sympathy and more action.

Girl, non-certificate, 'never belted'. On a scheme for unemployed young people at a local FE college.

I liked my school because of the warm freindly atmosphere. Most of the teachers are kind and understanding even although I was difficult and cheeky at school. I was supposed to take seven 'O' levels at school but I had no interest in any of them so I just mucked about and disrupted the whole class. That is one thing I do regret because I know the rest of my friends were

staying on at school and they failed a lot of exams they could have passed if they had paid more attention.

Girl, non-certificate. Packer in a textile mill.

I enjoyed my last year at school only because we didn't work very hard. I must admit the teachers were great they treated us as adaults and not school children. Our class's were smaller and to me this was great because I found the class could have a sensible disscuion with our teachers and even the boy's were sensible.

Girl, non-certificate. Packer at a paper mill.

I liked the teachers, well some of them because most of them would sit and listen to you, but others didn't, because they had a lot of work to do themselves.

What I didn't like about school was when you went into a class and the teacher wouldn't give you anything to do they would let you do anything you liked.

To help, young people, the teachers should explain things more clearly and listen to the pupils because some people are shy and doesn't like to admit they cant do there lessons.

Girl. O grades, no A–C awards. Warehouse assistant.

'They treated you like an adult'
appreciating adult treatment

I am now 17 years of age, I left school exactly 1 year ago. I enjoyed my last year at school. My teachers were most helpful, they treated you like an adult.

Girl, non-certificate, belted 'quite often'. Receptionist/telephonist.

What I liked about school was most of my teachers were young and I found them easier to talk to. The teachers did not give you a lot of homework because they thought you were young & should enjoy yourself. One of the teachers also took a number of us away for a week to do art which we thoroghly enjoyed. The school did not make you wear school uniform & most pupils wore what they liked I found this better. I did not know what appertice ship's for Platers, template makers were I think teacher's should tell pupils about apprenticeships. I have always wanted to go back to school to tell my teachers about myself

& to help pupils leaving school but could not get the time, and know you have done this for me. THANKS.

Boy. O grades, no A–C awards. Apprentice plater.

I think my school had very good facilities and I think the atmosphere of the place was good. I also felt the place had a well balanced level of strictness which included no commitment to uniform, being able to wear casual clothes at school helped to relax me. I must say I can't really think of anything I could say against my school. I am very happy at my job, it's interesting, enjoyable and I have good company.

Boy. O grades, no A–C awards. Apprentice electrician.

For my experience I found that most teachers just thought teaching was just a 9 o'clock till 4 o'clock job but I think that if you want to be a good teacher you have to give the pupils a little freedom and 99% of the pupils will respond a lot better.
What I didn't like about school was the teachers who tried to make you say SIR after you spoke to them and this caused a lot of trouble at my school. Of course, you get good and bad teachers just the same as you get good and bad pupils.

Boy, non-certificate. Apprentice mechanic.

In my last year, I liked how we didn't get so much work and the teachers treated us better, and it was a time to meat all your school mates. I didn't like like how some teachers still treated us like kids though the time was ok. but some teachers made it so boring but most of them let us play cards, quizzies or read plays.

Girl, non-certificate, belted 'often'. Unemployed.

At school the teachers are to interested in school uniform than in teaching subjects. If you say anything to put a point of view across which differs from teaches you are branded as a no good trouble maker.

Boy, non-certificate, belted often. Apprentice engineer.

When I was at school I hated every minute of it we were treated like stupid little kids. It was all work and never any enjoyment in it, the teachers gave you a book which you were to answer the questions and that was it never any class discussions about what we would like to do or what we did do outside school. I think when you go into a class and there's a different teacher he should talk to us more like an adult they always said we should act. He or she should tell us about themselves what they do

when at school and when not at school and he should ask us individualy what we do.
The rules are childish as well. no talking. in the corridor do not walk fast. do not put your hands in your pocket.
They expect us to act like adults but we were always treated like children.

Girl, non-certificate. On a work experience scheme in a hospital kitchen.

Dear Dr Joanne Lamb,
Firstly I would like to say that some of the questions asked require only a yes or no answer but I feel that some of them need more explanation. Secondly, I would like to know of any special reason why I was chosen to complete this form, as I know of no one else who received a copy. Also I think that some of the questions are put in such a way that a ten year old could understand rather than a seventeen year old, because this reminds me of the way I was treated at school. At Secondary school, I would like to see more pupils treated as individuals rather than being just recognised by their grades or ability. I think if pupils were told about different careers in their first year at secondary school they would have more time to make up there minds and choose a course on which to set their standards upon. Finally I would like to thank you for taking any interest in me and what I am doing. I apologise for the delay in returning the questionnaire.

Girl, non-certificate, belted 'quite often'. Assembly line worker.

'What would stop the children running riot?' alternatives to corporal punishment

I think being made going to assembly was bad because half of the people didn't like it. I liked our school because it was quite modern and in the language department we had all the up to date and also in the Science labratory. My personnal opinion is the belt should not be done away with because teachers would have no power across children and *I would like to know what would stop the children running riot and doing anything they want. Please let me know what would stop them doing this.*

Boy, non-certificate. Tractor Driver.

I would like you to hear what I say very much. What I liked at my school was the education and most of the teachers. What I did not like about school was the belt because I think there is a better way to deal with pests.

Girl, non-certificate, belted 'once or twice'.
Sewing machinist.

What I like about school was that you made new friends and got on with People you dident know who existed & you learned how to read & write & count which you need to know if you want to get on with life these days.
I dident like being forced to take subjects that I dident like or understand at High School. I dident have any thing against the belt as its the only thing the teachers had to keep us in line.

Boy, non-certificate, belted 'quite often'. On
a short industrial course for unemployed
young people, in the building industry.

I think the belt should be banned as well speaken for myself it did'nt do much to help what they should do is like keeping pupils in at interfils theyd soon chance their mind if that to happen.

Girl, non-certificate. Shop assistant.

The school was okay it was pretty modern with modern equipment e.g. In the P.E. department the vault etc where all quite new and there was all sorts of stuff in g.y.m. What I didn't like about the school was some of the teachers (NO NAMES MENTIONED) they tended to treat you as young children rather than adults and also the belt although I never had it when I was there I still think its childish to give the belt to 4th and 5th year pupils. In my opinion people would rather the belt was abolished and some form of other punishment was introduced e.g. detention.

Girl, non-certificate. Re-sitting O grades at
FE college.

I think Scotish Secondry School's are useless because they don't get involve with the pupil's I have been to two scottish secondry shcools and one English school and out of the three I prefer the last one because the teachers get involved they try to talk to the pupil's *freely* for instance if they were thinking of going on holiday (the school that is) they ask the pupil's where they would like to go, they don't *demand* anything from them. I was with three boys once and they got caught the teacher didn't give him a strap or belt. he just took him to the science teacher, and then brung out a smoking machine which inhaled the smoke etc and it showed you the proceed's of how it works, how you get far in your lungs they had cotton wool for the lungs and when the operation was finished he showed how BLACK it the cotton wool was from the CIGERATE this is just one of the many things

and ways the can help you. by the way the three boys that got caught smoking give it up after they seen the operation, and thats not a lie.
(Well I hope I helped a little).

Boy. O grades, no A–C awards. Metal worker.

I would have liked the teacher to have spent a little more time with me, but due to the overcrowded classes,
They didn't have enough time, The tension Showed,
on the teacher's face, when They Could'nt get Something Through to you,
because, of vast overcrowding She Couldn't Control
the lot of us, I Would have liked more freedon of Speech, to the pupils,

Girl, non-certificate. Unemployed.

I would like to have stayed on at school. I never really had use of my first years it wern't until my third year that I learned all the useful things. But by then it was too late. But now I have a full-time job and I would not leave it. The teachers at the school I went to just havent got any interest in these pupils. If the teachers gave us more hard work and had helped us with it I think girls and boys like me would stick in and get all there O levels and such things. I really enjoyed my last year at school because teachers could trust us and make us feel grown up and we never needed any of her help. She just stood and watched us if we made a mistake she would correct us not just jump up and wack us. I think that belting a pupil is no use. It just brings the worst out on them. If they do anything stupid they should be corrected and not belted. The belt should never be used at school because it just brings a bad influence on any child and they will just do it again and again.

Girl, non-certificate. Factory worker.

CHAPTER FIVE

'I LIKED BEING
AT SCHOOL BECAUSE . . . .'

Subjects and courses

I liked being at school because most of my teacher's had time to spare for us if we were having difficulty on a certain subject, they could also help in personal or home problems and this could be told in confidence. There is not much I did'nt like about school.

Girl. O grades, no A–C awards. Bakery worker.

Non-certificate leavers often discussed their curriculum in terms of their relationship with their teachers: '. . . in fact I liked doing any subjects in which I liked the teachers'. Leavers were grateful to particular teachers who took time to explain things, to those who did not expose individual pupils' failings to the class, to those who were evidently concerned that the pupil should achieve mastery of at least some part of the work and, again, to those who treated them as adults; though teachers' difficulties in meeting the variety of pupils' ideas as to what constituted adult treatment were possibly not eased by the sort of attitude expressed by one girl who said her class got on very well with the English teacher '. . . he was just like a Pupil and didn't think he was any different from US'.

Perhaps it is the importance of this personal element in the curriculum, especially when seen in the context of the themes of rejection, respect, authority and control that have emerged in the earlier sections, that explains why it is difficult to summarise neatly non-certificate leavers' views on what they were taught; whether and how they were taught were often more important. There was wide agreement on the importance of the 'three R's' and often regret when they had not been mastered, but they were not universally popular subjects. Some leavers did not get the remedial tuition they had requested. Others who were given remedial work sometimes resented the fact that they did not get the same work as others. Nevertheless, just under a third of non-certificate leavers indicated that they would have liked to have spent 'more time in their last two years at school learning to read better' and two out of three would have liked to have spent more time 'learning to do sums better'.[1] Academic subjects were rarely mentioned. Nor did social, religious, aesthetic or moral education loom large in what non-certificate leavers appear to have valued. Some girls resented the fact that practical subjects in their school had been provided on a sexually-differentiated basis. But many leavers had enjoyed their practical work, had usually seen it as 'practical' in relation to future career possibilities and had often wished that more such opportunities had been available. Experiences such as community service that increased contacts with the world outside school were almost always appreciated.

A small proportion of Scottish fifteen-year-olds in the later 1970s had the opportunity to spend part of their final year of compulsory education on courses 'linked' to a local FE college. Over a quarter of the non-certificate leavers in 1975/76 had been on such a scheme and the large majority had found the experience 'worthwhile' or 'worthwhile in some ways'.[2] Those who wrote about such experiences valued their improved status as students and their close contacts with the world of work. Pupils who wrote about the vocational education provided at school and about the help given with preparation for job hunting usually thought it offered more than just 'learning to say "yes" instead of "aye"'.

Leavers also appreciated schemes of 'work experience' when the school provided them but fewer than one in five non-certificate leavers had had this opportunity.[3] Some leavers were resentful that opportunities had not been provided, or that they had been prevented from attending: 'I would have liked to do job experience and you have to be in the lowest class to do so'.

Community service, link courses, work experience, vocational preparation and

[1] Further information on this topic may be found in Freeman and Staite (1978) and in A Group of Principal Careers Officers (1978).
[2] *Idem.* See also Raffe (1980c) for an evaluation.
[3] A Group of Principal Careers Officers (1978).

vocational training all seem to have provided contexts in which pupils and teachers could handle their relationship with each other and thereby keep open the possibilities for learning. 'If only the teacher could convince the pupils that the last 2 years are really important' wrote one boy who achieved only D and E grades, saying 'I only wish in the years to come people can get what we didn't get through our own stupidity'. The rigours of the world that await the school leaver may be a source of such conviction. A girl who had also achieved only D and E grades said 'only my O level classes did I enjoy, I only took 3, the rest of the classes I had nothing to do most of the time. Apart from PE and home economics. I think that in the classes where I did nothing should have been spent on prepareing us for leaving School and showing us what the world outside was like. When I left school and went to work. It was very different from school. At school there was not much discipline, I think there should have been more, and at work there is quite a lot of discipline, lack of discipline at school i think started me of on the wrong foot I thout work would be much the same as school and no one ever told me that it was not'. But she concluded 'I really do not think that there is much more can be done to help young people find jobs as there is not many jobs to get'.

It is against this background that schools must work out a plausible basis for a curriculum for the leaver who has little prospect of gaining certification that the labour market will value.

'I liked doing any subjects in which I liked the teachers'
subjects and teachers

In my last year at school I was treated as if I were more grown-up. I liked doing the community work best, in fact I liked doing any subjects in which I liked the teachers.
Girl, non-certificate. Data processor.

I enjoyed my last year at school very much, and I must admit that my carrers teacher was a very good help to me he seemed to take a very good intrest in what I wanted to do.
Boy, non-certificate. Shop assistant.

I like the sporting side of school PE was my faviorite subject. But I was never any good at my other subject's so my dream was out. I think we should be treated more like adults not children. College is more adult like.
Boy. O grades, no A–C awards. Apprentice engineer.

The teachers were very helpful and did their best to help you in every way. And that there were so many different activities. Some of the teachers didn't arrive in the class till about half way through the period finishing off their coffee.
Girl. O grades, no A–C awards. Employment unknown.

My last year at school was quite good but it was a waste of time becaus you didnt get bossed about as much as you did in first Second and third year and that ment you didnt have to go into any class you didnt like and We use to get quite a lot of free periods. Some of the teachers were very helpfull but others just didnt bother and the teachers that bothered were the teachers that took the subjects we were not very interested in the liked of Business Studie I was not interested in that but she wast the only one that tryed to help us on know I am working in an office which I said I would never do.
Girl, non-certificate. Office worker.

What I most enjoyed at school was my Modern Studies + English classes. I got on really good with both teachers & they were very helpfull. I know it seems funny about what I'm going to say next even though I now love my job in an office but I used to dislike my Business Studies classes at School. This was because I did not get on with my teachers & they were not even

interested in pupils like me. They paid all their attention to the girls who loved the subjects.
Girl. O grades, no A–C awards. Office junior on a work experience scheme.

At my school I liked their system in the choosing of subjects ie. if you chose a favourite subject and told them, then you could get the most of this subject as they would give you it more times than you would get any other subject and could realy enjoy it and their would be something to look forward to instead of thinking of going to dodge it because the subject was forced onto you when you were'nt even intrested in it.
The thing I did'nt like about it was teachers attitudes towards their pupils that wanted to learn. In our school teachers were more intrested in the ones that knew what to do without being shown what to do, they would praise them then move on to something different, while the ones that did'nt know what to do were still sitting there still puzzled about their last exercise frightened to say because they knew in theirselfs that the teacher either start shouting and embarrass them by pulling them out in front of the whole class but this would'nt happen in teachers showed more understanding.
Girl, non-certificate. On a community industry scheme for unemployed young people.

Well now that i have left school i have learned to look after myself and by whatever i need myself instead of my mother having to buy me everything. To tell you the truth i didn't really like much about the school i enjoyed some of my Lessons such as PE and English they were my favourite subjects because i never got bored in these subjects and Mrs _____ the PE teacher was very good she tried to encourage me and understood me and we got on very well together and so to was Mr _____ the English teacher he was just like a Pupil and didnt think he was any different from US. At work i find it just like school because people still think there higher than you and are always telling you what to do and what not to do.
Girl. O grades, no A–C awards. Working in a textile factory.

I enjoyed English because my teacher took time to talk with us and always answered our questions treating us as individuals instead of 36 pupils. Most teachers didn't care if work was understood or not.
Girl. O grades, no A–C awards. Fish net worker.

Everyone at school was friendly and I got on well with all the teachers. I liked all my

subjects. One teacher at school I liked best of all was my cookery teacher. You could tell her anything and she would keep it to herself, she told us some things about jobs and was helpfull.
Girl. O grades, no A–C awards. Works in a clothes factory.

I liked my last year at school because of the way the teachers understood and helped you if you wanted to know something that you didnt understand properley I didnt like some of the teachers, especially my French teacher because if I didn't understand any thing he would say he was to busy or he didn't have time to explain it to me.
Girl. O grades, no A–C awards. Office worker.

'Apart from the three "R's" . . .'
views on basic and practical subjects

Apart from the three 'R's' I thought school was a waste of time and did not cater for my needs. Although some of the staff were very helpful on a personal level.
Boy, non-certificate. Apprentice hairdresser.

The teachers were not very help-ful at all, except for one or two, who really took an interest in the ones that were in (B) classes, the rest of them were all for the girls and boys in (A) classes, the girls in my class would certainly have wanted to do better. But no-body had any time for us, as far as I'm concerned. We just felt we had been left out, and then the trouble began, we started carrying on in classes, and playing truant from classes. I never missed Maths or English as I really liked studying these subjects. To me the teachers that taught these subjects were the only ones who were really bothered, to teach us, even if they had to drum it into us day after day. (I was always pleased when we would get two periods of art, as I was quite handy with a pencil or brushes.) When I left school at Christmas, I was out of work for four months and my ambition was to be a nurse. So as I couldn't be a nurse without the qualifications I just had to take a job as a machinist. I think if the teachers tried a little harder with us my ambition would have been fulfilled. And I would be in a better situation now, if they tried the little bit harder, one or two of the other teachers did.
Girl, non-certificate. Textile machinist.

I am 16½ year old. I liked the high school but Wasn't to Keen on primary because in our p7 class there was 2 groups A+B. Well A was all them who were Brainy and B was for them not so. Me and my friends were in B and all we got was '10 a day' and cleaning cuboards and when it came to spelling we was told everything spells as it sounds but that isn't so in every case. I still cant do fractions. Some of my friends picked them up in there fourth year but not me or Janet there's probaly more of us. But at Secondary I liked it because the teachers were more helpful. I never understood Science or mathematics I dont think I ever will. I was sad to leave high school because I Really liked it. And it is really depressing when you dont have a Job when you go for interviews for Jobs and dont get one you think you'll never get one. Usually its because you've no 'o' levels but mabey the person without o' levels will be better than the one with so they shouldn't go by that Really they should test you first.
Girl, non-certificate. Unemployed.

I found some difficulty at school, and could not keep up with the rest. For this I was put into a lower class, so that I would get a chance to catch up with the rest. However I found this did not work this way. We were left with nothing to do and we got *7 a day* to do, this is what they get at the primary school, they did not care about us. However things are working out well for me and I have learned much more now, and doing very well.
I think when boys and girls find a job and they have only a few weeks left to go to school, they should be allowed to leave and start in this job.
Boy, non-certificate. Apprentice mechanic.

There were some subject that I licked at school and were (1) Science. I licked science because I licke to work with chemicals and study the sells and diffrent sorts of stones on the shore. (2) Uropean Studys. I like d Uropean studys because I was able to study Urope and talk diffrent lanuges. There were some subjects that I dident like at school and they were mathamatics and arithmatic because I dident get the same work as the rest. I never got the chance to do any of the same work because I was backword. And when I went to a special teacher I never got the same work. I was getting work from the primary school.
Boy, non-certificate. Labourer.

I didn't learn anything at last year at school. I asked my English teacher to give me spelling lessons because I wasn't any good at spelling but she didn't bother I think it was because it was the last year.

Girl, non-certificate. Jute mill worker.

At school I liked cooking and sewing and all practical work But did not like English and things like that.

Girl O grades, no A–C awards. Textile worker.

At first I would like to say I think this book is a good idea to find out the facts about school to be quite honest I dont think sec. school does much good because you learn what you need know when you leave. I suppose the important subjects like English and Arithmetic help you but subjects like Latin & History they are all past it the present & the future young people want to know about. I also think that most schools should have classes to show pupils how to go about getting jobs and where to go. Well I hope I have helped you and I have found it very interesting.

Girl, non-certificate. Clothing machinist.

Theyr'e is only one thing that I didn't like about school and that was Arithmetic, I found it quite difficult, but it helped me a lot because I work in a big shop and my buyer will be retiring soon and I think I will be asked to become buyer and Arithmetic is something that you must know about.
I wish I was back at school because you didn't need to stand on your own too feet, and you had no worries, and it gave you a chance to meet people, now a day's I never see any of my friends because I am too busy.
I think that work experiance is a good thing, it gives younger people a chance to see what shops are like, I only wish I had the chance.

Girl. O grades, no A–C awards. Shop assistant.

My father is foreman of the work I work in. I am in his work, serving my time as a Welder, I do like it. I go to college one day a week, but I only wish I had more maths as I need it now, because I get calculasons and I have been there for ten months now and I can not do them yet.

Boy, non-certificate. Apprentice welder.

I am working now as an Office Junior and my boss is being very kind and consideret. But he is only going to give me a couple of more chance's then he will have to put me out. Because I don't now my tables and I am a terabble speller as you may have noticed. He is putting me into day release for Mathes and I am going to _____ College 2st a week (evening).

Girl, non-certificate. Office junior.

The only teacher I got help from was my sewing teacher Miss _____. None of the other teacher's helped. They never gave me homework because they all knew I was leaving, they were only bothered in the one's who were staying on to take 'O' level etc.
Im glad Ive left school making money and meeting people. Im also learning a trade. The only subject that helped me from school is my sewing also part of my maths. But most if what I got didn't help. Ist year French then I never got it again, things like that. Im happy in my job, but I miss my friends from school thats all I miss about school. I think Im better working.

Girl, non-certificate. Apprentice kilt maker.

My last year at school was quite good as most of the teachers I had were good and taught you quite well. My favourite subjects were history, art and PT. At school the only thing I didn't like was having to go to assembly every morning.

Girl, non-certificate. Unemployed.

The things I liked about my school was that if you had problems the teachers were always there to help you no matter what it was. What I didn't like was they gave you periods of music and drama when you could have been doing more important subjects in that time which may have helped you more.

Girl, non-certificate. Machinist in a tailoring business.

I have been interested in cars since I was a boy of Nine and I think I could have been helped in my last year by books on that subject or some other practical way which I think would have helped me now that I am a Apprentice Mechanic.
I like my job its interesting and varied and it will get more interesting as I get some more experience.

Boy, non-certificate. Apprentice mechanic.

I would like to have left school at least a year before I was allowed to, because I was not learning anything that would help me very much in what I wanted to do after I left. I cannot fault my teachers they were only doing and teaching as they had to what I found wrong was the fact that unless one was clever at English, sums, etc., there was very little else. I would have preferred more work that involved the use of my hands. I would have taken great pleasure in my schooling if I could have been trained or had some learning in Motor Mechanics. Too much time is spent on the 'brainy' people and not enough time on others who do not want to do anything academic. I got my job by writing to all the garages (about 12) and finally was given an apprenticeship with _____ and have passed my City and Guild (Stage 1) with Credit for written work and Distinction for Assignments.

Boy, non-certificate. Apprentice motor mechanic.

I think School gets better around 4th year, because you were allowed to do more, eg. Metal work, in first to around 3rd year in Metal work you were not allowed to use the centre lathes in Science you were not allowed to do as big experiments, I think pupils with a certain ability should be able to choose 'O' level subjects that they want to do. The best thing about school that I liked doing was Technical subjects.

Boy, non-certificate. Miner.

I wasn't at school much in my last year but when I was there, I liked Art and Arithmetic very much because my teachers were understanding and spent time on helping and listening to you. I didn't like Geography or French or anything like that, because I didn't think I would have any use for it, I would rather have done mostly bricklaying and painting and things like that which I never had the chance to do. I worked in a coachbuilders after I left school for 4 months, and then left as I didn't like it. But now I am back in another coachbuilders, but I am getting on a lot better. Also I don't think it is right that most of the jobs are offered to people with O' levels rather than people like me, I think half of the jobs nowadays is nonsense about haveing to have O' levels for a job, sometimes maybe but mostly never. I think that most boys and girls that I know are better workers than those with O's levels. I hope this is useful if you get any good jobs with money let me know. Ta.

Boy, non-certificate. Coachbuilder.

The thing I licked moust about school, was technology Drawing and Woodwork. I lick woodwork becouse you were allowed to make what ever model the class vote to make. eg. Tables, boles, Lambs. I did not like art or music becouse I was not very good at art. and we only plade tapes at music. I lick English becouse we got filing in form and doing thing that would help you when you left school. I did not find any thing difficult at work asept building at first. I think there is plenty off shemes to help young people looking for jobs. eg work experience, job creation, short industrail course, training workshop.

Boy. O grades, no A–C awards. Apprentice builder.

I am 17 and I liked school very much. I did not think there was anything wrong excep that the pupils shold get a chance at all the subject in the 1 & 2 years instead of all the boys doing wood work and metalwork and the girls doing cookery and sewing. both should get a chance at each subject and I also think they should pick the course early in the year.

Girl non-certificate. Taking a secretarial course at F.E. college.

To help young people who are looking for a job they should be taught more worthwhile subjects. They should be told what to expect when they go out to look for a job. And there should be less discrimination in schools. Girls should be allowed to take any subjects they like and they should be encouraged to take subjects like, woodwork, metalwork and technical drawing and things like that.

Girl. O grades, no A–C awards. Typist.

I liked school. I was in a class called community service. It was to do with people. We went on visits to lot's of diffrent hospitals, old people's homes, children's home's. At cooking we were shown what kinds of meals to cook for small children and old people. Every Wednesday morning, instead of going to school, the whole class went to diffrent hospitals or nursery's. If you were at a nursery you would play with children, and look after them. If you were at a hospital, you talked to the people, and helped the nurses. That was the part of school I liked best. The other things I did no school were English, Maths., Cooking and Social Studies. There was nothing I did'nt like about school. I had great teachers. But now that I've left, I would'nt like to go back, working's better. I didn't have any trouble getting a Job, my teacher phoned up for an interview for me, I went up for it got the Job. It's a sewing factory they make uniforms, As for people trying to get jobs. I think less qualification's should be needed for some jobs. Like nurses. Someone without o grades, could make as good a nurse as someone with them. You dont need o grades to be good at a job. Just some training and you could be just as good at the job.

Girl, non-certificate. Clothes machinist.

Thank you for sending me this form. I was very glad to answer your questions. Well, I enjoyed my last year very much. I was involved in a lot of things e.g. I was in the youth club looking after kids two mornings a week then on Thursday afternoon I looked after the old age people and I enjoyed it very much and I got very much attached to them all and didn't want to leave them I did that till I started work with

_____. I worked there for 4 months and I really hated it and wanted out because all I was doing was putting bottles into boxes and stacking the boxes. It was good money but I count stand it any longer so I packed it in and so far I have not been able to find a job since then. But I have been looking. I do not want to go into a factory. I'd like to work in a clothes shop or a baby shop but my real ambition is to try to get into hotel work. But I would go back to school on a tick if you got payd for it. But not to worry something will turn up I hope. Your welcome.

If there is any further information please do not hesitate to contackt me.

Girl, non-certificate. Unemployed.

'The teachers taught us like students'
taking courses linked to colleges

I was not at school for the last year I was doing a course at _____ Technical College (Agriculture) it was great. The teachers taught us like students not like children as they do in the schools. I dont like the way the teachers were teaching bottom classes at our school they would give us something to write down and get on with there work they were doing for ther classes. They could have given us more practical work instead of a lot of book work, plus given more attention to the bottom classes. I have worked as a chambermaid in the _____ hotel for 3 months. Then I was out of a job for 3 weeks until I got a job in a waitress in _____ where I still work just now. But as I told the Careers Officer before I left the School to go to College for the Course to see if he would look out for a job as a farm labourer for me but I had no luck I am still looking for that job that I like best I hope this information helps you a lot.

Girl, non-certificate. Waitress.

I would just like you to know that my last year in fulltime education was at college and not at school. I found I was getting nowhere at school At college I got the qualification which helped me walk straight into a job. I do have one regret about college and that is, I did not pass my O levels. Although I only sat two (All that was possible in the course) I felt that we were

not being properly coached for them. However, I am quite happy with my job and qualifications.

Girl. O grades, no A–C awards. Office junior.

I didn't like the way that when you reached the age to take O grade's and you didn't qualify for them all you went to classes and did nothing and classes that you did get work in, if you couldn't do the work you didn't get any help. In my last year at school I really didn't get much work at all. I used to get sent to the school office to answer the phone and help any visitors with enquire's.

During last year I attended _____ Collage of Technologe and did a course on Hairdressing and Nursing. I passed with a B grade for both subjects. I was one of the lucky one's when I left school as I knew someone who worked at _____ and they told me there was a job to get if I wanted it. I had a few relations who worked there and my employer knew we were good workers.

Girl, non-certificate. Clothes machinist.

I think the school leaving age should be dropped to (15) years old, because the last year I was at school was a waste of time. going to classroom's and being told the same old things over and over again, not only was I bored but it was an awful waste of money. wasting new jotters and buying new books for us. I was only at the school for the first six months of my last year because I got a coarse at a technical college to give me an idea of what I was going to be doing when I left; Before I went to the college I had a job at a garage part-time after taking the coarse, I got a fulltime job. I think this is a good idea if younger people get a chance to make use of that stupid last year at school to see and learn about what he's going to do for the rest of his life.

Boy, non-certificate. Motor mechanic.

'Say "yes" instead of "aye"'
getting ready to look for work

I got good advice. The Careers Officer told me to write to shops. The housemistress taught me to speak properly in interviews, to say 'yes' instead of 'aye'. The typing teacher taught me to write letters.

Girl, non-certificate. Employment unknown.

In my last year it was interesting as you were trying to get jobs, going for interviews, and you were allowed a little bit more freedom, and fun. I didn't like Arithmetic in my last year as it was all just revision, though I liked P.E. and Secy. Studies. I don't think my teachers could have been more helpful, as they helped you get interviews, and helped you write letters for jobs.

Since I left school I have worked in an office. My job includes—Typing Orders, Filing, doing the Mail, sometimes standing in for the Telephonist, and general office duties.

Girl, non-certificate. Office worker.

My last year at school was good. Because the teachers treated you like adults and they help in every way to tell us about finding a job. That we liked. Telling us what it would be like to starting a new job and all the difrent things about the jobs showing us film on finding job and all the dificult thing you find in a job. Please execuse the writing and the spelling.

Girl, non-certificate. Factory worker.

I think my last year at school was quite useful because, the teachers gave you some idea of what it would be like when we left school, and they didn't tell us it would be easy to find work. At school they taught us how to write a letter enquiring about work which is very useful because if it was'nt for the teachers I would'nt know what to write. When I first left school I was'nt all that keen on finding work but once you realise its a thing you've got to do, and when I realised it I could'nt get one, But I'll keep trying.

Girl, non-certificate. Unemployed.

My last year at school was very good school wasn't really all that bad I suppose it was just getting up early. At the last year at school we didn't have to wear a uniform and it was great as I think uniforms are a waste of time. I was in non-certificate as you'll maybe no I could have taken o'levels but my friend's didn't so neither did I I am glad now becouce the earlier you leave school the more time you had to look for a job. Mr _____ who started IDE started a good thing this progect was interesting you took photographic work made baskets etc you learned usefull things. We went to the Industrial Instatute for 8 weeke it was like a factory I think thats what helped me the most you see I got sewing there, and it helped me get a sewing job.

Girl, non-certificate. Clothes machinist.

The last couple of years at school were the best because you got to like the teachers better and

some of the helped you to find out all about the different kind of jobs you could do and what job would suit you best befor we left school we got took round a textile factory to see what like it was and we got told all about it. how much you got what time you started and finished it before they took me round that company I looked for a job myself and I found one I went down for an interview and they tried me on they machine at that I was took back to the office he told me I was quite good and I could start as soon as I left school. But I got the other job because it had more money and it was nicer and tidier.

Girl, non-certificate. Textile machinist.

I thought my last year at school was most enjoyable because we were treated better and we had better teachers. Most of the teachers we had would listen to any problems the class had. Not all the teachers but most of them. I didn't agree with the work we received at school The teachers just gave us something to keep us occupied. We were just left alone. The time could have been more useful if the teachers had asked what we wanted to do when we left school and given us a course concerning the job you would like eg. office work—a business study course.

Girl, non-certificate. Taking a secretarial course at FE college.

'Aim for something in life' preparing for work

I like the school because you meet a lot of people. I like meeting people and making new friends. I try out anything I haven't done before. The school tried to make aim for something in life.

Girl, non-certificate.

What I liked about my school was that almost all of the teachers are really keen on teaching you something. What would be a great help to people at school is, 'if only the teacher could convince the pupils that the last 2 years are really important. I think that almost everyone who leaves school with no grades at all regret that they didn't try hard enough and allways wish they had enother chance. If the teachers could find a way to convince pupils the importance pupils would maybe start leaving school with a few 'O' grades to help them find a suitable career. The only difficult about getting a job is the fact that you don't have the suffcant qualifications.

I think that all people leaving school should have a chance to go into an apprenticeship. Which I am convinced is the highlight of any male schooleavers live. I only wish in the years to come people can get what we didn't get through our own stupidity.

Boy. O grades, no A–C awards. On a work experience scheme.

My experience was that any pupils who were not taking any O' levels were only at School on Sufferance, with the teachers showing little or no interest in them. I think there should be more vocational training for such pupils as opposed to academic work.

Boy, non-certificate. Apprentice blacksmith welder.

I just think is the last 6 months thay should take you into collages and show you some works and help you get a idea of what a job is about By this it can give you a more idea what is like doing the job etc.

Boy, non-certificate. Apprentice glazier.

Since I have left school I have been very happy. I have been lucky enough to go into a good trade which I am very interested and good at. One of the things I liked about school was I had a good bunch of classmates. One disadvantage of school was the teachers took things too seriously.

I think that when you do into your third year at school they should have more scheme's in the school for people who are leaving at the end of their fourth year, so that they know what they are up against when they leave school.

Boy. O grades, no A–C awards. Apprentice upholsterer.

Some teachers really pushed you with your work and wanted you to pass your O' grades, but others dident bother. I get on well at work, and I thought that I'd have to have an O'grade in needlework to get the job, but I dident. I think they should have more day releases in schools, at our school, it seamed to be only boys who went on day releases. Even if the schools should try and work out a scheme for pupils so they can taste the sort of job they'd like, before going into a Job they dont know what its like.

Girl. O grades, no A–C awards. Clothes machinist.

The best thing about school was meeting friends and joking about with the teachers. I didnt like the subject's and thought it was a waste of time and the teachers just didn't want to know you if you weren't interested. No experience. that's what is difficult about looking for work and no qualifications. They should be allowed job experience (like my sister who's in 4th year and she go's to a shop on job experience) but when I was at school they wouldn't let me do this as I was in an O' level class and it was only the bottom class that got to do this. I had no ententions on sitting O' level's and asked if I could move to a lower class but they said no. I would have liked to do job experience and you have to be in the lowest class to do so. I just really hated school and couldn't wait to leave.

Girl, non-certificate. On a temporary community service scheme for unemployed young people.

When looking for a job the school should let pupils go *more* than *one day* a week for work experience in thier last year if employers are willing to take them.

Boy, non-certificate. Porter.

I did not like school much. I liked some subjects like cooking and biology. I dislike all that moveing from one room to another and that if you fell behand the teacher does not try to help you. You have to ask friends to show you what you have missed and how to do it which sometimes does not help you much.

I have found when I have interviu you are nervos and the employer sees this, and you don't know what to say.

I think there should be a scheme where boys and girls in the last year at school should be able to try a job which they want to be when they leave school so they know what it is like and if it is for them or not.

Girl. O grades, no A–C awards. Unemployed.

In question six you ask about being on a Job Creation Scheme. I would like to point out that I started the Scheme in the January and was then employed by the Company in the June.

I feel this Company has given me a lot more experience than I did from School.

I think that School does not prepare you enough for work or going out into the 'big wide world'.

I must point out that I was supposed to sit 7 'O' levels, but thought at the time I had no chance of passing.

I feel that School is not personal enough & tends to revolve around discipling the Pupils. Instead of trying to understand the Pupils and give them the necessary help, & advice.

I think that a Schools could maybe start a scheme where pupils in their last year at School could maybe go out one morning, afternoon or even a day to an office or a Shop for more experience. The same of course would apply for boys. I hope I have been able to help you in

some way
  Girl, non-certificate. Office junior.

Any Way there is one thing I apreciated about
the school in my fourth year I got day release to
an offfice this really helped alot when I went
for a job because I could say I had experience
in working in an office also the boss in the
office I went to thought I would really do great
working in an office as I had done so well there
and he gave me the phone number of his office
and said when you leave just phone in here if
you need a refrence. I find that some girls are
very nervis about going for an interview for a
job I think it would be a good idea in school to
have more actual interviews they could even get
the boys and girls to act out interview to give
them more confidence when it really becomes
the time to go for an interview for a job.
  Girl, non-certificate. Clerkess.

I liked secondary school in my first and second
years. because there was work to do in all my
classes but when it came to my third and fourth
year and it got very boring. only my o level
classes did I enjoiy, I only took 3, the rest of
the classes I had nothing to do most of the
time. Apart from PE and home economics. I
think that in the classes where I did nothing
should have been spent on prepareing us for
leaving School and showing us what the world
outside was like. When I left school and went
to work. It was very diffarent from school. At
school there was not much discipline, I think
there sould have been more, and at work there
is quite a lot of discipline, lack of discipline at
school i think started me of on the wrong foot I
thout work would be much the same as school
and no one ever told me that it was not. I really
do not think that there is much more can be
done to help young people find jobs as there is
not many jobs to get.
  *Girl. O grades, no A–C awards. Factory
  worker.*

CHAPTER SIX

'I AM GETTING A WAGE EVERY WEEK'

Working life

I did'ent realy like school at all, I think I'd rather work, because I am getting a wage every week, and meeting new people, finding out things I did'ent no. I havent realy found enything difficult at work, as I am shown alot.

Girl. O grades, no A–C awards. Office junior.

Nine months after leaving school in 1975/6, the majority of non-certificate boys who had found work had done so in semi-skilled or unskilled jobs. Only a handful entered white collar work and around one in ten found skilled employment. Among non-certificate girls, about one in ten found a white collar job; a further two entered service work as, for example, shop assistants or hairdressers; and another four took up manual work largely of a semi-skilled nature (such as clothes machining).[1] Leavers wrote about their problems in finding a job and a job that they liked, about the pleasure and drudgery of work, the new disciplines it imposed, about starting again at the bottom, getting on well or badly with their work mates and being used, in their eyes, as cheap labour. Those at further education colleges were often pleased at their unexpected success or pleasure in the course.

[1] Further details may be found in Raffe (1980a). Note that this analysis combines those with 'no awards' from O grade attempts with the non-certificate pupils who had not presented for the SCE.

'I was thrown into something which I did not understand'
preparation for the transition to work

When I left school no one told me anything about the social security, jobs etc. I was thrown into something which I did not understand and had to find out about myself. If the school leavers of 1979 were still as confused this year I would not be surprised because no time is taken to explaine the details of school leaving to them. During my last year at school I found it interesting in O level subjects and a complete waste of time in others I think the age for school leavers should be 15. The present age for school leaving is an easy way of reducing unemployment for the goverment.
Boy. O grades, no A–C awards. Labourer

I have found nothing difficult at work, But I found that when going for an interview I got nerves and did not know what to say because I hardly go much about interviews at school. And I found that a lot of jobs were looking for more older people and people who have had some experience before.
I think that schools should talk more or even act out an interview not just write about jobs But to actually act them out and I think schools should have more work experiences even if it is just for a day, I think before people go for an interview he/she should have a talk with a person who knows something about job hunting and give them some questions on what an employer would say to them. I think that would give them more confidence.
Girl, non-certificate. On a training workshop scheme for unemployed young people.

For young people who have just left school and looking for work there should be courses for them to learn how to handle interviews and how to fill in applications as well as how to go about getting a job.
Girl. O grades, no A–C awards. On a work experience scheme as a sewing machinist.

Dear Dr Joanne Lamb,
When I left school I thought it would be straight into a nice job, But I was mistake. I had to work hard to get this job and I think it is not realised with people about to leave school. So I think schools could be improved by explaining more clearly how difficult it is to get

a satisfactory job after leaving school. I didn't really enjoy school, it was the people in it I liked. Sorry I took so long for this to be returned but I took time and thought about it. Yours faithfully
Girl. O grades, no A–C awards. Office junior.

I think people who have not long to go in school should be allowed to go out and look for jobs a few month before they leave school. Also they should be allowed to go to employment offices, careers offices etc. to look for work when they are still in school.
If I were still in school and just leaving soon, If I did not have a job I would stay on in school.
Boy. O grades, no A–C awards. On a work experience scheme in a garage.

'Its not a bad job but I would like better'
getting the right kind of job

well to start with, I went to work and was started by working on a cutting machine. In the work we make bags Jute bags, Poly bags. Well now I am on the _____ it's a machine which turns jute bags. I get a shot on feeding the bags into the machine. It's not a bad job but I would like better.
Girl, non-certificate. Machinist.

My job is not very good but it was the only one i could get, I looked all around it was trying to get a job as a motor mechanic but I couldn't get a start at any garage. Then I got a job in a beer bottling firm as a van boy, just delivering the beer not very good prospects but it gets me some money.
Boy, non-certificate. Van boy.

Since I left school I spent 5 month looking for a job around my area. The job center found me a job on one of the job creation systems, untill I found myself a job in [chemical company] as a labourer. I worked there for 3 month but left because I did not like the work or the people I worked with. I started at _____ steel works and worked there for a week as a sample carrier, I left because I got offered a job as a mechanic in [engineering works] which the job center found for me. At present I am at college backed by [his firm] but looking for a new job as the section I work in is shutting down.
Boy, non-certificate. Mechanic.

The thing I liked about my last year at school was when we have someone from both the army and the merchant navy visit the school. They gave us an idea what it would be like in both these careers and I found both extremely interesting. I didn't like being left in a classroom with nothing to do as it became very boring and this is why I think so many people play truant.

My first job was as an apprentice butcher but I did not like it, also the pay wasn't to good. My next job was semi skilled machine operator with an electrical engineering company. I drill holes through metal and other materials. We also make a lot of goods for the national coal board. I like my job very much.
Ps Sorry for delay.
Boy, non-certificate. Engineering machinist.

During the last three months of school I had a part time job so I wanted to leave as quick as a could to go into my job full time. I left school on may 31st 1978, I started work in June. I started in my job as a sales assistant, I then was a cashier, the before a left I was head Cashier The next April I had a disagreement with the manageress so I left. I am now unemployed.
Girl, non-certificate. Unemployed.

I think as soon as people have done one year at the academy they should be shoan films about different jobs so they cane make up their minds and stick in at the subjects they need for the job they are most interested in. I think they should try and make classes smaller. so that the more backword child could have more attention. I think they should have a better system to help people revise for their exams than having to do it all at home. Subjects that they don't get until they are in third or fourth year. i.e. Accounts, Sec Studies, they should give them and introduction earlier or to let them know that they are about before they go picking them as 'O' grades and then wish they had n't.
Girl. O grades, no A–C awards. Factory worker.

The most thing I found difficult at work was, getting myself to speak to all the customers in the shop because I get easily embarrased, at the least thing. To help young people to-day they should go on a week to the Laity centre with the school, I think that really helps you alot, you get told whats its like in Interviews + they get all different types of people from different jobs to come + tell you about it, its really Interesting and that helped me a lot.
Girl. O grades, no A–C awards. Shop assistant.

My name is _____ the thing I didn't like about school was that they didn't tell you enough about what a big step their is from school to work. You have got to get on with people and you have got to be responsible in your work.
Boy. O grades, no A–C awards. Apprentice joiner.

I am 16 yrs Old and I am an office junior & TELEPHONIST. I enjoy my work very much. I didn't like school at all in fact I hated it. I think that the school should allow you to go for interviews and help you look for jobs during school hours because I didn't get much help or advice when I was at school about looking for a job. and when it came near to the time that I was to go about it, it it wasn't for the careers officer, i would still be looking for a job. She helped me a *lot.*
Girl. O grades, no A–C awards. Office junior.

I think the there should be more people to give advice in schools besides the careers officer, as I didn't see the careers officer until the last year of my schooling, although I was lucky, as my careers officer was able to tell me more about the course I wanted to do. But not everybody gets the chance. So there should be more frequent visits from careers officers, than just once in four years of schooling. And there should be more schemes eg. working experience in schools so that pupils will know what to expect when they eventually leave school. I think instead of 1 subject that you pick before going into fourth hear they should give you the chance to get working experience in place of a subject.
Girl. O grades, no A–C awards. Taking a course in nursery nursing.

My job is dirty cold in the Winter. There's no central heating, in fact there is no heating atall. My father got me the job, and as I could not get a job elsewhere I took it. But I don't think I will be there for very long, I am looking for a job this minit. But I will not leve my prescent job if I don't get one.
Boy, non-certificate. Welder in blacksmith shop.

When I left I got a job straight away in [clothes manufacturer] but I didn't like it, no one would talk at the break, I left _____ at the beginning of December and I have been looking for a job ever since.
Girl, non-certificate. Unemployed.

Well I do not like my Job at all. Since I left school I have done machining, and every day I go in, I am looking for a different Job In the yellow pages, I am phoning them up without any luck. I regret not studying in School because I could have done it if I tried.

Girl, non-certificate. Clothes machinist.

'I like my job very much'
enjoying work

I have one job as one APPRETNCE baker. I like my job very much and I work with Pastry I do quit a lot of jobs. The best job is making Doug Nut.

Boy, non-certificate. Apprentice baker.

I was offered a job in the _____ Hotel just after I left school and I like it. I did not have to go on the brew or out looking for work. I have found nothing difficult about work. Making beds is easy and so is carrying trays. Well when I first started I was a waitress and was shown how to serve all the different foods but it is easy now. Then I moved upstairs to the bedrooms and waitress in the afternoons. I enjoy my work very much. I don't know what should be done about the unemployment because I do not know how they feel, I have never been on the brew.

Girl. O grades, no A–C awards. Hotel worker.

I am now working on a dairy farm doing all farm duties from milking to ploughing and thoroughly enjoying it all. I go to the Young Farmers Club regularly where we get a wide variety of demonstrations and lectures.

Boy, non-certificate. Farm worker.

I worked as a van boy for I while I enjoy that I like travelling around the country. I am now working as a bricklayer, I like this because I am outside.

Boy, non-certificate. Bricklayer.

Since I left school over a year ago I have been a lot happier in many aspects. I find myself more responsible moneywise and for the first time in a few years I have been interested in doing something worthwhile. I love my job and have never regretted leaving school and personally I think school leaving age should be 15 not 16. My last year at school was of no help at all and I learned praticcally nothing. I feel that my last year could have been more useful to me if I had been allowed to be employed. Right now I am very happy, and I am looking forward to my apprenticeship ending.

Girl, non-certificate. Apprentice hairdresser.

I am still working on the same job getting up at 5.30am and milking 187 cows in byres, when the milking is finished I wash the machines and pipeline, (where the milk go's through). Milking is finished about 8.20am. After I do the dairy I go and make the breakfast for my dad + 3 brothers I look after the house cook all meals, do washing, etc. I do alot of outside jobs, e.g. sweep up byres and yards, put horses outside and (cows in summertime), fill barrels of straw and hay, fill coolers of barley, drive tractor occasionally, move cattle, feed cattle, paper work. At night I do the milking again and finished work about 8.00pm. I have a border collie he does not like boys and is a very good worker with cows. My dad has some clydesdale horses, and sometimes takes them to the shows. He has five entered for a show in May.

I liked having cookery at school the teacher I had in 3rd + 4th year was really good. Some of the teacher were boring and unhelpful. The economics teacher never explained anything about the subject unless you asked him. hope this is O.K.

Girl. O grades, no A–C awards. Describes herself as 'farm dairy maid'.

'My work was terrible very boring tiring and monotunis'
the drudgery of work

When I first went out to work I did not have a clue what it was all about the work was terrible very boring tiring and monotunis If I told you and explained what I was going into I dont think I would have done it I think you should be shure of what you are doing when you leave school it is a very big step to take. now I work in a hairdressing salon and love my work it is so different from the factory I think I have been very lucky having had a second chance and I hope a lot of other people have it too.

Girl, non-certificate. Apprentice hairdresser. Formerly a clothes machinist.

The only thing I found difficult when I first started work was having to do the same thing over and over again each day. Going out to work for a living isnt as exciting as most people think it is. I am afraid I dont know what should be done to help find young people who are finding it hard to find jobs, as I had no

difficulty in finding one. I think they are doing all they can at this moment.
Girl, O grades, no A–C awards. Watch assembler.

Since I've left school I have held 3 jobs. Each of these I found very boring. My present & 3rd job involves sitting sewing 1 little straight seam approx. 100 times a day. As you can imagine—boring. My reasons for staying are; money and the present job situation i.e. I could not find another one.
Girl, non-certificate. Clothes machinist.

Since I left school in December I have started work in the _____ [clothing factory] I like my work very much which is piecework because it's quite interesting, and has a very friendly atmosphere. I was one of the lucky ones because I only waited two weeks for a job.
Girl, non-certificate. Clothes machinist.

I spend my last year at school doing a lot of subjects as English, Maths, typing, Cookery Sewing and P.E. and I enjoyed my last year at school.
I am working in _____ [clothing factory] doing sewing sides to back.
I enjoy my work at _____ and I bing there for 8 months.
Girl, non-certificate. Clothes machinist.

'When your working you have your head down all day'
the discipline of work

When I left school at first I thought it was great, But after a couple of weeks when I was left sitting in the house I began to get Boared I used to sit and think of the days I scidged school and got off so easy but now when your working and want to take a day of you lose a days wages and may even lose your job, I think when your in school and taking O levels etc the teachers have more time for you as for myself I didn't take any and didn't think there was much doing, school would be great if there was more outdoor subjects. I always wish I was still in school because when your working you don't have the same inrests and get lonley with no one to talk to Because you have your head down all day.
Girl, non-certificate. Shop assistant.

When I was at school I liked most of the teachers and the way you would take a day off without thinking about How much money I would lose. I didn't like the way they kept on about what o' levels would do for you, as I know quite a few people who got o' levels and are still out of work. Since I have been working the thing I find most difficult is getting up a lot earlier in the morning, and not getting so much leasure time and activities.
Boy. O grades, no A–C awards. Apprentice welder.

Working now you know that you have to get up in the morning, because you get pay for it. If they pay you at school every body would go, they would not stay off one day. Working now you learn a lot more than you did at school. When I was at school I was alway waiting for the bell too go. When you are working you meet lots of people and go out, but at school you were staying in to study. You don't have to study when you are work now.
Girl, non-certificate. Kept on in a clothes factory after completing a work experience scheme there.

I liked about school changing to classes for different subjects and dident have to stay in the one class all day. I liked some off the teachers in school. I liked when I was in 4th year because you could sit in the assembly hall I liked going to Art Classes. I have found out that you have to come to work at the write time and cant sit and talk.
Girl, non-certificate. Working as a textile machinist in a government training workshop.

When I first started work I didnt mind it but I found it a lot different from school you cant turn round and say thats not fare the way you could at school. You cant be off not well without a sick line. You cant have time off work without making up time, but like everything else you get used to it.
Girl, non certificate. Worked as a chambermaid but left because 'to early a rise (sacked) and to much on bus fare'. On a work experience scheme as a shop assistant.

What I liked about school was making pals. I hated school because I found it boring and not very exciting and it was of no use to me as the Job I am in I don't need any O levels or anyting all I need for my Job is speed. I found my Job very difficult for the first month or so as I could not go at the same speed as everyone else but then after a coupla warnings about getting the sack I somehow picked up speed so now I have been working for over a year so I am quite happy.

Girl. O grades, no A–C awards. Electrical goods assembly line worker.

You cant stay of when you have a cold (HA, HA, HA).
I enjoy my work I meet lots of new people everyday lots of people come in to chear you up, get a good laugh with them. they are just good to get on with. My work mates are all fine the'll help you we all help one another.

Girl, non-certificate. Shop assistant.

When I left my first job (job creation) and started my apprenticeship it was differant from what they told me about at school. It seem to be stricked in some way about filling in time sheets. As an instance you have to put every job you were on even if you only helped someone for a couple of minutes.

Boy, non-certificate. His first job was on a work experience scheme as a shopassistant. Apprentice mechanical electrician.

'I am the "boy" of the shop'
starting at the bottom

When I started work as an apprentice butcher I expected to be working with meat straight away but not I have found that I am the 'boy' of the shop and that I have to do all the small jobs, but not after more than six months they are begining to show me how to 'bone out'. I really am enjoying myself now and hope to do almost everything.

Boy. O grades, no A–C awards. Apprentice butcher.

I dont get on very well with my employer ever since I started he has been nigling me, I was working with him myself one day and we have to travel around a lot, he said he would pick me up in the morning but he never turned up, so I got 3 buses to the job I was going to and when I got there he was there I asked him why he never picked me up in the morning, but he said he was there and I wasnt. Then I looked at his face and I knew he was lying. I was going to hit him but I would have lost my job, so now I find my own way to jobs.

Boy. O grades, no A–C awards. Painter and decorator

I am very pleased with my job as I stand. I really did stick in a lot a school for the simple reason I know if I did not make an effort I would not be in the job I am in to-day. I was very lucky indeed to get into such a good job under CSE Basis. But when I was 12 years old I use to work on a Saturday morning for them helping them with the stamping of the holiday brouchers. Then now and again I would learning some bits and pieces on the running basis of a travel agecny clerkess. I really put my own way out in showing I was keen to do the job even although some of the things I was told to do was a bit scarce. I just let them see I was keen to learn and was willing to learn the skills. This is what brought me up to standard to-day with my clerical assistance job. I am not just a the one job all the time, sitting at an office desk with a typewriter. I also deal with reservation and lots more to do with airlines sales retursn etc. Thats the main thing about my job its not a job you can easily get sick off because everything can be done in you won time as long as you know it will get done.

Girl. Sat CSE examinations.

I work in a large _____ store in _____. I dont like it very much as I find it very hard to get on with all the Managment it is all completely different from school; I can say I am a good worker and never stay off. But they dont care how they treat you as ther is always someone to take your place; but then again I dont mean I would like to be a pet.

Girl. O grades, no A–C awards. Shop assistant.

I didn't like school very much.
I wasent very clever at school but I managed to get a job straight after leaving school.
The only thing I liked about school was PE and the holidays.
The thing I find difficult at work is being the youngest and having to do the bad jobs.

Girl, non-certificate. Shop assistant.

I liked sewing at school by hand and machine I also liked gymnastics and all sports. I think young people should try to help themselves first before asking other people, they should also know what they want to do I never really had any problems getting work or at work except my first job. But a manager has no right to hit anyone. The job I have suit's me fine I have good work mates, enjoy my work, and good wages.
Yours sincerely

Girl, non-certificate. She left her first job as a clothes machinist because 'I had an argument with manager after he bruised my arm with a punch'. Now doing the same work with a different employer.

I didn't have to wait long for a job because I had forms in the factory 5 months before I left school. The job I have is quite good, a lot of my friends work beside me and I get on good with my supervisor. I am a sewing machinist and we make all sorts of clothes mainly for girls.

Girl, non-certificate. Clothes machinist.

I have a smasing job that I like very much I like the people I work with and I am not getting told off all the time, As I am at home and school.

Girl, non-certificate. Waitress in a large hotel.

'I get on well with everybody in the factory'
good or bad relations at work

I like my work I get on well with everybody in the factory is just ½ mile down the road. It is in a small village called _____ It is a friendly place you get to know everybody. The wages are not bad you get a free overall I have been in the factory nearly a year But as for school I was glad to leave.

Girl, non-certificate. Assembler in umbrella factory.

I work in a small garage and I have found no difficulties at all since I started work. I have a friend my own age working with me plus good relations with the older men that sees us playing football together at dinnertime. I had no real difficulties in finding a job because I looked for one two or three months before I left. I got one and was ready to start work but even although I was asked to leave the headmaster would not allow me to go saying I had to stay to the leaving date in December. If I hadn't got a job I would have stayed at school. I think everything is being done to help school leavers. its just that there are not enough jobs for everybody. Maybe lowering the retirement age would help.

Boy, non-certificate. Apprentice in a coach-building workshop.

What I find most difficult is keeping up conversation with the customers. I feel if I chat to them about the weather etc. they'll think I'm silly because I'm only a 'wee girl'. Also if a customer comes in and I ask if I can help them sometimes they just ignore me and go up to one of the other *older* assistants because they dont think I'm capable enough. I could say a lot

more but I cant think of it all at once, sorry about the writing. I'm in a hurry. Yours

Girl, non-certificate. Sales assistant.

I didn't have any difficulty in finding a job. I would rather work in a factory that i would in a shop or a Supermarket because I am not very good at counting and i couldn't stand the thought of trying to count up numbers in a shop and a big queue waiting to get served, because i would get all frustrated I work in a factory that makes babywear and i hear lots of stories about people acting bigheaded towards you since you have Just started but i found that it wasn't like that at all. All the girls are very nice and no one has yet tried to bully me and i have made a lot of friends. I think that there should be job oppertunity's for people who are finding it hard to find a job or at least every employer should employ one person to give him or her a chance to learn something.

Girl, non-certificate. Sewing machinist.

Since I left school I have completed a ten week course on secretarial studies at _____ College of Further Education. I have had a job in a sewing factory which I was very unsuited to and I am now in another factory which I don't like.
The factory I work in is very unrefined. The people I work with, or most of them, are very tough and rough spoken. If I had a choice this is not the kind of job I would be working at. I personally think the reason why school leavers and teenagers are having such difficulty in getting a variety of work is because far too many women who have worked, married and have had their families are now back working in the jobs we should be doing.
These women should be made to retire between the ages of 45–50 to give school leavers the chance in life they had.

Girl, non-certificate. Packer in a food factory.

1. The only thing that I liked about school was that I had all the friends in the world. but since I left, I have no friends at all, and now I feel like killing myself. I am not telling you this to get sympathy, it is just the way I feel about life.
2. Then there is the inability to cope with work, people nagging you, swearing at you, blaming you for things you didnt do.

Boy, non-certificate. Worked as a painter's labourer on a temporary basis. Apprentice butcher.

'Childs pay'
low wages

I find it difficult at work:—when I started at
_____ [textile manufacturer]. I was
very keen on work and found it great and did
my work fast. but after a few weeks I slowed
down. Therefore I was told off for not going
fast enough and that I was holding up
production I feel that if your only getting half
the pay of an 18 yr. old upwards you should
only be expected to do half the work. Therefore
if they wish you to do a man's work they
should give you a man's pay. I was for the past
five month doing a man's work and only getting
a child's pay. Now I have been shifted to
another job in the firm. I am quite satisfied
with it.
   *Boy. O grades, no A–C awards. Works in a
   textile factory.*

When trying to find a job I found that it was
hard to get one not unless you were 18 or over.
Now I am nearly 18 I find I am to old to look
for a job because the bosses say there looking
for a young person.
I am in fact a commis chef and I find that
working in hotels it is under paid and you work
more than 50 hours a week and get paid about
£20. I think that the bosses now are to big at
thinking if he doesn't work the hours that he
says then they sack you and when you go to
another job and find that you have been sack
then they do the same. I would like to tell you
more but I have run out paper.
Yours sincerely.
   Boy, non-certificate. Commis chef.

I have not found anything difficult about work,
I seem to get on good with everyone. I think
there would have to be a lot more jobs
provided. The other thing is young people are
not willing to work for the little money
employers are paying them because they don't
think it's worth will, because about £20 does
not go far these days.
   Boy, non-certificate. Warehouseman.

I found my job in the papers went for an
interview and got the job. A small business, I
do plumbing & electrical work although when
at Technical College I only study plumbing
electrical work I learn off workmates.
I dont like doing jobs I shouldn't be doing in
my job like taking out stones from walls
building in fireplaces and some other jobs
which people should be doing The Bosses get
this money to themselves in which we get just

our usual pay These jobs would help other
people to get work as far as I am concerned it is
just greed.
   Boy, non-certificate. Apprentice plumber.

The Job I am doing now is my first Job since
leaving school although I like my Job, being an
apprentice the wages are not very good,
although I know when my time is served I shall
be on a very good wage, I think most firms and
other Employer's who employ apprentices
should have something of an incentive for
apprentices as I have nearly been on the verdg
of giving up my chance of a trade through other
employers giving better wages to labourers and
other workers while I have only a small wage.
Yours faithfully.
   Boy, non-certificate. Apprentice car-sprayer.

Now that I have left school and I am serving
my apprentiship I find it unfair that students
get exempt from tax and apprentice do not.
Students get grants for books, but apprentices
don't get grants for tools as that is what most of
my spare cash has to go on.
   Boy, non-certificate. Apprentice plumber.

I an fortunate to have a job as an apprentie
Painter & Decorator—I received no instruction
on this trade at school, yet I will make
eventually a good wage from this trade—When
my 'time' is out I believe I will be earning more
than my teachers at school.
   *Boy, non-certificate. Apprentice painter and
   decorator.*

There should be more Apprentice-ships for
young people. And They should not leave till
they are 17 when they are well-educated—
Because when they start work at 16 and get
payed I think it drives them all too drink, not
out of of sales, but in pubs.
   *Boy, non-certificate. Unemployed, formerly a
   metal cutter.*

'I didn't just go to college to stop me from having to work'
non-certificate leavers and further education

What I liked about school was that in my last 2
years I started to realise that I wouldn't be
there forever and I would soon be out working
like the teachers and that they wern't there just

to make my life unbearable. When I started to
look for a job in my last 2 months at college it
was difficult it didn't matter if you had
qualifications it was experience that they
wanted, well as they wouldn't let me sit any
"O" grades in school I felt I would like to go to
college to get them and I was lucky that I was
accepted because there were a lot who were not.
I didn't just go to college to stop me from
having to work I done it to better myself. Well
now I'm in a good job. I started as office junior
and now I'm a cash clerkess. which means I'm
counting a lot of money so it's not all fun it's
responsibility too.

Girl, non-certificate. Studied for O grades and
secretarial certificates at FE college. Office
junior.

I would like to say I am very anxious about
getting work, but I felt my last year at school
did not prepare me for work, so with my
parents help I decided to take a Secretarial
Course at _____ Technical College. I
know I have learned a great deal more there,
and now that I have almost finished my course,
I would like very much to get an office job, but
I am most apprehensive knowing that most
firms want applicants with experience. I would
really appreciate the opportunity to work and
do it well, but it becomes very difficult when
no one will give the young people a chance to
try and prove themselves. I think what happens
is that some young people are lucky and get a
job soon, others unfortunately get turned down
or aren't offered anything so many times that
any confidence they have in themselves fades as
the time goes on. I sincerely hope that someone
will give me a chance.
Yours sincerely

Girl. O grades, no A–C awards. Taking a
secretarial course at FE College.

At first when I started secondery school I hated
it. Then third and 4th year were really great.
When I was in my last day Before I left I wrote
away to go to college to study residential care. I
never thought I would get in because I have no
O'levels. But when I working down in
_____ I got a letter telling me I was to go
and sit an entrance exam. I went back down to
_____ and I got another letter saying I
had passed my exam and was to go for an
interview I got in because I had the right reason
because I had no qualifications. college is *great*
but I don't get paid. I do get a bursery which
helps.
Goodbye & Thank you.

Girl, non-certificate. Previously a canteen
assistant.

I am very happy at college doing my catering
course, I have to study hard as I want to do my
best, and get a good job when, and if I get my
Certificate. I was very happy at my High
School, where I had a lot of good and also kind
teachers.

Boy, non-certificate. Trainee chef.

I am a good worker and I stick in quite well. I
like the teachers and I like the catering course I
am on and I also like the way we get more than
just one subject.
Young people looking for jobs should go to a
College of further education and try to get some
more further qualifications to be sure of getting
a better job and getting up in the world as
that's what I am trying to do and I have found
it very helpful so far as I am getting on really
well where I am.

Girl. O grades, no A–C awards. Apprentice
catering worker.

I am a 17 year old student, I find my course
Preliminary Residential Care very interesting. I
espicially enjoy practical placement which
involves going to nursery, primary schools and
special schools. (In first year).

Girl. O grades, no A–C awards. Studying at
FE college.

I did not like anything about school, you are
always treated as a KID who doesnt know its 2
times table, you have to sit and listen to a
teacher all day which you may think is the same
as being at my technical college but there you
get payed for it and you are not treated as a kid
but as a sensible young teenager.
Since I started this course I think that I have
learned a great deal more than I would have
learned in the same course at my old academy.

Boy. O grades, no A–C awards.
Apprentice joiner.

I enjoyed the first few years of my secondary
school but my forth year was very boring. I
think a lot more pupils would enjoy school if
you did not just read books and take notes. If
teachers taught in a more friendly manner and
made the lessons more interesting everyone
would be much happier. I also believe that
schools should have classes showing the pupils
what work is all about just like sex education.
When I left school I knew I had failed my
exams because I was overcome with nerves and
I did not know what I wanted to do, I felt I
was not ready to start work so I went to college
and I must admitt I love it, much more than
any year at school. I have just received my mid-
term report and I have A passes for every exam;
this is a big difference from school would'nt
you say so. I am still rather scared of starting

work but I guess that's part of gowing up. I would like to write more but there is not much room. I hope I have been of some use to you and if possible I would like to hear of the outcome of your survey.

Girl. O grades, no A–C awards. Studying for O grades and secretarial certificates at FE College.

I got four O grades when I left school, But, unfortunately they were not passes and this meant that I couldnt get a good job easily without them as they are essential nowadays. I also had a chance to go to the local college which I considered before leaving school. However, to get a place in the college you had to get a C, B or A in English O grade which I didn't. But, I was considered, and as I had just failed they let me in. I am now nearly finished the course and I am awaiting my exams in June. I am sitting 3 O grades again, plus my college certificates. (typing, English, shorthand, office, practice, and Accounts). I had good marks in all my subjects at my christmas exams, and I am progressing satisfactorily. I think young people (without certificates) should be able to enter a course like this and sit for their O levels again, or more or different certificates in these college. They should be able to come out with a satisfactory amount of certificates with will enable them to get a job. Not attention is giving to these people when leaving school, the govt training scheme does not offer certificates.

Girl. O grades, no A–C awards. Studying at FE college.

I am attending the _____ College. I have been there since I left school last year. The course I am doing is a City & Guilds Bakery and Confectionary course lasting One year. When I left school I thought college like would be good, but I was wrong, for, the mere fact they still treat you like children and anyway, I dont like baking, or decorating cakes. This is why I have said I would like to be a steward.

Boy. O grades, no A–C awards. Apprentice baker.

I enjoy my work verry much I have been at college one day a week for the past year in december of 76 I had an exam to sit it was CITY + GUILDS PART 1 BASIC ENGINEERING CRAFT STUDIES and I past with credit. My first six months with my firm were spent with FABRICATION INSPECTION AND FITTING. My next six are as follows 3 MONTH IN MILLING 3 MONTH IN TURNING. After that the manager of the training centre gives you an Interview and you choose which module you

would like to take now I am in turning 2 for 6 month and Engine fitting for 6 month then I will move up to the _____ factory and train to be an engine fitter or turner.

Boy, non-certificate. Engineering worker.

I left school in 1975, DEC, and started work with steel company in Feb 2nd 1976 and I have been working there since. It is a four year apprentice ship and I go to Collage one day out of every week. I am a Mechanical Engineer (Maintenance Fitter) When I am doing my work I need to read Technical Drawings and do calculations, and also metal work.

Boy, non-certificate. Apprentice mechanical engineer.

CHAPTER SEVEN

'NO VACANCYES'

Unemployment

I feel terrible without having a job. The reason for us young ones not having a job is because of the older generation. Every week I go to about 5 jobs and I am told there is no vacancyes. What else can I do.

Girl, non-certificate. Unemployed for 9 months.

Unemployment among young school leavers more than doubled in the five years from 1972. Between the time they started at secondary school and the time the non-certificate leavers of 1975/6 entered the market for jobs, the proportion of all unemployment borne by the 16–17 age group almost doubled to around nine per cent.[1] Within this age group unemployment was concentrated among those with very low examination qualifications and those with none at all. Table 6 shows that, in January 1977, about nine months after the majority of 1975/6 leavers had left school, the unemployment rate was just under a quarter among non-certificate leavers, being 24 and 23 per cent for boys and girls respectively. But it was only eight per cent among those who had attempted O grades and it was under five per cent among Highers leavers. Further analyses of these data by a group of Principal Careers Officers has shown that, within the group of O grade leavers, unemployment was directly associated with low SCE qualifications. For example, leavers who had attempted O grades but had achieved no A–C awards had an unemployment rate of 12 per cent, whereas those who had achieved three or more such awards had a rate of around five per cent.[2] Non-certificate school leavers, and those with only marginal SCE qualifications, were therefore bearing a disproportionate share of the general rise in the level of unemployment in the later 1970s.

Nine months after leaving school, half (49 per cent) of the non-certificate leavers were in their first job and a further fifteen per cent were known to have already changed jobs. Fifteen per cent had held a full-time job but had left or lost it and just under one in ten (8 per cent) had been continuously unemployed since leaving school.[3]

In the light of this situation, it is not surprising that the writing of the non-certificate unemployed expresses depression, bitterness, boredom and hostility at a situation of 'no vacancyes'. One boy, unemployed for nine months, writes 'I have been looking in most every place in _____ for jobs and I still haven't had a job. Sometimes I sit in the house with nothing to do and other times I go out with my friends who are also on the dole. When we go about the streets the police usually pick us up for know reason at all. Some people thing we are to lazey to work but little do they know. In _____ we have a shopping centre which I have also tried for a job and there's none. I was over at the shopping centre a week back and they had a notice up on all the windows saying there were jobs only for university graduates coming out of university for theyre holidays. Its alright for people at university they get a thousand pound grant of the government a year so they can come out and be well off and because I am bottom class I am never offered jobs and 9 pounds a week to buy fags, clothes, food, footwear etc'.

What did non-certificate leavers find difficult when looking for jobs? In response to a fixed-alternative question just over half mentioned 'finding out about jobs to be had' and 'knowing which you would like'. Three out of ten mentioned 'filling in forms' and four out of ten indicated 'talking when you met people who could give you a job'.[4] Persistence was important, and morale: 'Somewhere, Someone is wanting a young school leaver'. Suggestions for improving their lot included a variety of measures for sharing work more evenly and, realistically or not, the view that more jobs should be created.

[1] A Group of Principal Careers Officers (1978)   [2] *idem*
[3] *idem*. The remaining 7 per cent comprised 3 per cent who were not seeking employment, 1 per cent in part-time work, and 3 per cent in full-time employment but for whom the number of jobs were unknown.
[4] *idem*.

Something like this was one of the purposes of the Youth Opportunities Programme begun in 1978 by the Manpower Services Commission to co-ordinate various existing *ad hoc* measures to reduce unemployment, and also to introduce a number of new elements. The programme has had two main thrusts: 'One is based on Preparatory courses which are intended to upgrade the vocational, academic and social skills of unemployed youngsters; whilst the other is based on the development of a number of Work Experience schemes based on employers' premises, specially devised projects, Training Workshops and Community Services. By providing experiences in these fields it is hoped that youngsters will enhance their self-confidence and self-respect, improve their motivation and maintain the ambition to gain and hold a permanent job, when the opportunity offers itself or is offered.'[1] Leavers' reactions to the schemes provided under the programme have been generally appreciative. Where there has been criticism it has focussed on the low differential between the wage paid by the scheme (£20.55 in 1979) and the money paid by 'the brew' (social security). Some writers thought their employers had used them as cheap labour. Others however regretted that their involvement in a scheme could not have been longer. Early results from the 1979 survey of leavers in 1977/8 indicate that the schemes have been successful in other respects too: leavers who attended them were more likely than were other previously unemployed young persons to find jobs, and to do so irrespective of whether or not they had attempted O grades or achieved any A–C awards. (Raffe 1980b).

In this sense the Youth Opportunities Programme seems to be realising an ardent wish of many non-certificate leavers. 'Scrap O levels and make everything equal' was a commonly expressed view among non-certificate leavers, whether employed or not. They were deeply sceptical of whether SCE O grades in fact certified the qualities that were required for the jobs they were seeking: 'I don't really think you need O levels to be a tradesman as it never happened in days gone by'; 'Just because somebody has got more O levels then you does not mean to say that he is a better worker'. Others felt that, even if SCE O grades did certify something of value, leavers should be given an 'equal chance with the people that might be brainier than them when leaving school'. All in all, the view that employers were using leavers' certificates as a convenient but unfair and invalid, means of screening applicants for jobs seems to have strengthened the already very negative views among non-certificate leavers as to what education was all about.

[1] *idem.*

'Depressed and . . . demorilized'
being unemployed

I like for there to be more jobs available for young people, but instead as I experienced myself I made the medical with an older lady just the two of us and she was married, and she got the job and thats happened a few times to me alone, likely more people and the worse is their coming from jobs into other jobs and people who are unemployed don't even get a look in, it disgusts me. I've to find something before May and I've tried so hard for 4 months and I've got nothing if I can't get anything I get put back on the dole and when I was on it I was depressed and I began to get demorilized. I think you're doing a good thing.
Girl. O grades, no A–C awards. Clerkess/ typist on a work experience scheme.

I am unemployed at the moment but as soon as I turn 17 I am going into the army. the thing that I liked about school was the people in it and some of the things that I did in school. Cookery, games, modern studies etc. The thing I didnt like at school was some of the teachers. I have have found looking for work difficult because where I stay their are factories but they dont need any one I have tryed shops etc. but have had no luck. I thing that most factories should give young people a change of a job by paying more married women off who already have a husband working for them so that us young people might have more change of getting a job when we leave school.
Girl, non-certificate. Unemployed for over 3 months.

Since I left school I have worked in _____ Distillers Ltd 3 times and also the _____ [clothes manufacturer] but these jobs have only been Temp. (6 to 7 weeks) the teachers at my school were not very helpful about jobs or anything else like it. In a way I'm glad that I left school as I hated it most of the time. But I hate when I haven't got a job as I get dead *impressed* in the house everyday of the week. But I get the housework to keep me busy most of the day as my mother works as well.
Girl, non-certificate. Unemployed for 7 months.

After I left school, I got a job soon, I seen a vacancy write in a shop window and I wrote away for it. But when I finished that job, I found it difficult to get another. But I kept looking in papers and going to the Job Centre. I wrote away for another Job in a skill centre, for 8 weeks and I had to wait 6 weeks before I got in, I have finished their, and now I have to start looking again. That is the only way to get a Job, is to keep looking for one.
Boy, non-certificate. Unemployed.

In the last years at school the teachers could have given you something that could have linked up with a job that you would like to go to. Looking for a job is not a very pleasant thing to do. You walk round all day looking and asking. It is not very good for your moral when everybody seems to be saying no. The worst thing about looking for a job when you leave school is signing on the dole every week. It is a very degrading thing to do. All the jobs you see advertised are all for experienced people or over 21s.
Boy, non-certificate. Apprentice, specific trade unknown.

I have been looking in most every place in _____ for jobs and I still haven't had a job. Sometimes I sit in the house with nothing to do and other times I go out with my friends who are also on the dole. When we go about the streets the police usually pick us up for know reason at all. Some people thing we are to lazey to work but little do they know. In _____ we have a shopping centre which I have also tried for a job and there's none. I was over at the shopping centre a week back and they had a notice up on all the windows saying there were jobs only for university graduates coming out of university for theyre holidays. Its alright for people at university they get a thousand pound grant of the government a year so they can come out and be well off and because I am bottom class I am never offered jobs and 9 pounds a week to buy fags, clothes, food, footwear etc.
Boy, non-certificate. Unemployed for 9 months.

There isnt going to be any jobs for school leavers. If there were less strikes the more products the more money the more money the more products and the more money we could create more jobs. *WE NEED A BETTER GOVERMONT.* English get the best of everything scottish get the shit. The better the teaching the better the country in the future. But to have this we need a Better goverment.
Boy, non-certificate. Unemployed.

If I knew I was going to be unemployed for so long I wouldn't have left school. I think the school's should set up a number of jobs while still at school, maybe for 4 weeks or 6 weeks to give some experience to pupils and to let them see what it is to be like working. Because trying to find work without qualifications and without experience is very hard, I have found it very difficult trying to find a job as I have been unemployed for 5 months, with no experience at all.

Boy, non-certificate. Unemployed after finishing a seasonal job in a hotel.

Dear Sir/Madam,
I never liked school properly because no one ever payed much attenstion to me because I was a bit backward the only thing I was good at was Writting and I never even got any encouragement with that I feel if I had I would maybe of been more equipt to go into the World without a proper educastion now I have no prospects for a job all I do is sit in a house all day and do housework I used to go out looking for a job every day when I left the school but I am now so discouraged I coutlened Care less I think there should be a lot of little factorys or Centres made or turned into places for young girls or boys so that we could work together and earn a little money and be independant.
Thank you.

Girl, non-certificate. Left her first job for health reasons. Unemployed.

Well I liked school when it was intresting and if you had the write teachers. I liked art and typing. I would have liked to have worked in a office when I left school but we hardly ever got typing so I didn't know much about it. I have found it very difficult to find a Job I have had quite a few interviews for places but I have been no good or someone better has come along. I think that all the people that advertis should not need experience people and not only be wanting people about 20 overward. I think they should give us a chance because they would find out how good we really are. Well I cant really say anymore except if you know anyplace where I could get place write, and tell me as I am must about driving myself up the wall with being bored.

Girl, non-certificate. Unemployed.

I had a job in a sawmill in _____ for a short while but I lost my job I worked at a saw with another man and I put Rubbish on one belt and Good wood on another. I have not much to do with myself at home ther is not much to do in _____ I am Pleased that you send this to me it gave me something to do at home.

Boy, non-certificate. Unemployed for 10 months.

I think young people are underestimated just because they have no qualifications but there employer will be teaching them things thats new to them. What I mean is if you have qualifications or not your still going to be taught the same way. I didn't really like school because the teachers looked down on you as little boys, not as equals. What I did like was the sporting facilities. I am sixteen and I'm very keen on sport. What I want to do is, firstly an apprenticeship thenwill enable security for me later in life. Even long distance lorry driving I have always wanted to do that. The trouble is after writing for jobs and going for interviews and being unsuccesful you loose heart.

Boy, non-certificate. Laundry worker.

'Looking for work is really hard'
finding a job

Looking for work is really hard, I think the most difficult part is at interview, you probably get so scared you mix up all your words I think they should have groups at night for them to go to, so they can learn how/or what to expect during interviewing or how to fill out application forms, and how to speak on the phone to the man or woman who might become your boss. In other words how to show as good impression so that they may be impressed and imploy these young people who are just out of school.

Girl. O grades, no A–C awards. Office junior.

My name is _____ and I left school at 16 yrs. old. Since I left school I have found it difficult to find a permenant job as there are so many other school leavers with 'O' grades and highers who get more privelaged to the jobs, as many of them need 'O' grades, or prefer 'O' Grades. My advise to school leavers is (1) try to get into the collage. (s) try and get an apprentiseship in anything (3) put forms in to employers before leaving school if you can't get a job. go back to school but keep trying. As for me I sometimes wish I was back at school as its a better life then claiming unemployment benefit so be sinsible and if you can't get a job stay at school.
Yours sincerly

Girl. O grades, no A–C awards. Factory worker.

When I came out of the army I didn't get the job I wanted. So I took a job for seven months until, I got the job I always wanted. While I was working in a store I kept on trying to be bricklayer, trying every building firm in town, and by trying waiting for seven month, one of the firms I kept going too, took me on because they know I was keen for a trade.

Boy, non-certificate. Apprentice bricklayer.

I worked in a trapaulin factory for 3 weeks. And I was working part-time on a milkvan when I was working in this factory as well. Because I had worked on this van when I was at school for 2 years then their full-time milk boy left and so I packed in my job in the trapaulin factory and I worked in the milk for nearly 10 months full-time then the two girls who drove the can's and their mother decied to retire as it was their own busisness and it was one of the girls who got me the job in the OFF sales.

Girl, non-certificate. Shop assistant.

I didnt really like school, I have not found work difficult at all I like it. To be quite honest with you. I think there are plenty of jobs going, some of my friends say that the can't find a job but when I was wanting a job I got one. You can get a job if you try hard enough. I am an example I have walked out of one job into another.

Girl, non-certificate. Shop assistant.

The most difficult thing I find when being interviewed is that I find it hard to speak in a conversation I am shy.
I think to help other people find jobs is the careers officer they should be more helpful. I go over to the careers office once a month I go in as the woman says name I tell her then she says sorry nothing for you today. Two minutes and It is over. I think they should at least make out they are helping people.

Girl, non-certificate. Went on a short industrial course 'caring for people', then worked at a printers; unemployed for 5 months at the time of writing.

I did find it hard to get work when I left school. After a while I got a parttime job once I took this job I felt I had no hope of getting fulltime work. I did not do very well at school as I did not like it. I played truant often because I would not go to certain classes. I think you people should be able to get work if there were more jobs avaibale and the creers officers are not much help because every time you go to them they don't have anything for you.

Girl, non-certificate. Worked as a part-time waitress before becoming a shop assistant.

When I left school there were a lot of people looking for work, so you didn't really stand much of a chance of getting the job, and when you did get as far as an interview there were usually about 20–30 people there. The Careers Officer try's to help you get a job but she can't really make jobs for you. There isn't really anything that can be done to make jobs for young people looking for work cause etc jobs just aren't there to give them. It's not just young people that are unemployed it's some people who have worked most of there life and cause there factor is closing down.

Girl, non-certificate. Works in a soft drinks factory.

Some of the things i found difficult about Starting work were the forms that had to be filled in and also the people whom I had to notify of my starting work. I think Someone should have an office where young people who have started work can go to and chat about their problems. I don't think parents are much help here. Well my parent's weren't.
The best advice to any school leaver is to look around factories and so on for themselves, but also keep in toutch with the job centre and the careers office. I understand the problems these people have catering for so many unemployed people I hope other people also understand.

Boy. O grades, no A–C awards. Unemployed after leaving a farm job because he 'disliked the type of work'.

I am at present in a job which I dislike, I do apply for others but find so many are after too little jobs. I think it is most disheartning for anybody and just wish someome other than my mum or did + family would take an interest.

Boy. O grades, no A–C awards. Foundry operator.

For a start finding a job isnt all that easy. Because the Bus fares you have to use to get to the jobs. especially when you have no money. I think social sec should give everyone more money to help with these bus fares because it can sometimes stop you from getting a job.

Girl, non-certificate. Unemployed.

What I did not like about looking for a job is that every job I went for was taken just before I got there.

Boy, non-certificate. Van boy.

The silly thing about getting a first job is that the interviewer will ask you is you have any experience in that type of job eg hairdressing— impossible as it is an apprenticeship taken up when left school. They ask for your name+address Write it down and say they will get in touch when infact they put it in the bin.

Girl, non-certificate. Apprentice hairdresser.

For young people looking for work I think its a waste of time really going to Job Centre's because when you see a job you would like to do, there is allways about another 6 people going for the same job. I also think that employers should advertis more for young people instead for asked for older people. When I was looking for jobs, I went to this shop up town when they asked me were I stayed and when I said _____ [large council housing estate] they turned round and said could phone back, so when I did they just said that thay had some one else for the job.

Girl, non-certificate. Shop assistant.

The most difficult part of looking for jobs is the scarcity of work. More work should be made available in the highlands so that a job can be more easily obtained.

Boy. O grades, no A–C awards. Works in a clothing factory.

'Somewhere, Someone is wanting a young school leaver'
persistence in finding a job

I have now been working for six months, I like some of the work, but sometimes it gets a bit boring. At school I liked some subjects especially the practical work—woodwork etc. I did not like accounts and some teachers. It was hard looking for work, and at times I thought of giving up and just living off social security. But my advice to school leavers, is never to give up trying. Somewhere, Someone is wanting a young school leaver. So with a bit of luck and a few letters sent off to the right people some school leavers will have a chance to secure a future for themselves. I have enjoyed filling this in and thinking about my school and friends I had at school and I hope I have helped you in this survey.

Yours sincerely

Boy. O grades, no A–C awards. Shop assistant on work experience scheme. Would like to be a joiner.

I left school in May 1978 I wasnt 16 till _____ August 1978, so I had a good few months to look for a job. It wasn't easy not easy at all. I

wanted a trade something I could learn that would be useful not just any old job. My father has a trade and I wanted to have a trade too. I looked around went to all the building sites, in town. I even went to one building site 7 weeks in a row. Even then I never got a start. It was through a neighbour I got the job I'm in now. He told me they were looking for apprentices, so I went down next day and was told to start the next week. I got the chance off apprentice slater or plumber, and opted for plumber, I glad I'm working now and like my job very much. Its better than being on the dole, your out every day and time passes quicker when your doing something and you don't get bored. I don't get a great wage just now. But when I've finished my apprenticeship my wages will be quite good. I'm hoping to go to day school for further training in plumbing soon. This is through my job. And I will have to go at least once a week.

Boy, non-certificate. Apprentice plumber.

What I found really sickening was the attitude of some place's you went to look for work they treated you as if you were a nothing and I bet that put a lot of young people of working before they started.

As for careers service they got me one interview along with another 80 boys, and I understand they can't make just one person a special case. I was lucky I got myself a job and what I done was phoned up about 40 garages and out of them I got 3 interviews and I got one and if I was to give anybody advise about looking for a job it would be if you think an employer is interested just keep on pertering them to show them you are keen.

Boy, non-certificate. Apprentice mechanic.

I am now 17 I love my job but it took so long to get it I thought I would not get this job but I soon found out that you have to keep trying very hard. I thought it would be easy to get a job when I left but soon found out it was not as easy as that.

So my advice to people who is just leaving school is dont think it is easy to leave school and work just like that because you have to be the pick of the bunch at an Interview. I hope this is what you want to hear because this is what I feel and what I have done.

Girl, non-certificate. Previously worked as a clothing machinist. Trainee Cook.

To help people find jobs I do not know very much about because I found myself a job, but their careers officer is best because even though I had a job she still asked me if I was sure about it and said if I had problems to come and

see her.
Boy. O grades, no A–C awards.
Apprentice joiner.

I find that geting a job is not easy because there arenot that many about in _____ bus I am hoping I get a job in a farm My Careers Officer is trying his hardest to find me a job but there is nothing going I find it very boring through the day The only thing I do is go down town and look about for a job.
Boy, non-certificate. Unemployed. Previously a van boy—left because it 'was getting too hard for me'.

As for looking for a job, I don't think there is really enymore you could do for young people looking for a job it really up to them self to look for one. I think that the careers office is very good they help you alot, they explain how to go about looking for a job what to do, what not to do. It was them who arranged for an interview for me, and thats the job I'm in just now. I also went to a job centre which are a good help. Also Private Agency.
Girl, non-certificate. Clerkess-typist.

I am going to college at night for typing and I am sitting exams next month. I like my job very much and I did not have any trouble finding one. I would advise young people to keep going to their careers officer as I done. Often or every day and to keep looking at the paper at night also going to the Job Centre every day as my mum came with me.
Yours
Girl, non-certificate. Junior clerkess.

I found it hard to get a job at first, and when I got my first job I really hated it but I really like the job I have got now. I think it is up to the person to look really hard and not leave it to their careers office.
Girl, non-certificate. Left her first job in a bakery because 'did not like the work I was doing'. Office junior on a work experience scheme.

When I left school I looked for a job. I was just taking the first one I got so I tried for about 4 weeks then I gave up looking for one. I just sat about the house after that. So one day—it was a Tuesday—I got right fed up with sitting about so I went up _____ factory for the second time. He asked me a lot of questions and asked me if I was willing to work I said Yes. When he told me to start on Monday I jumped for joy.
Girl, non-certificate. Factory worker.

'Young people who are looking for work should be given a chance' suggestions to help unemployed youth find jobs

I think that young people who are looking for work should be given the chance of a job e.g. let the older people retire *early* so that young people can get the chance of their jobs. So they can learn a trade, and get a good job with good wages & prospects. Also good working conditions.
Girl. O grades, no A–C awards. Unemployed after completing a work experience scheme.

They should be abell to leave at 15 years old and They should be more jobs for them instead of bulding houses, they should buld facterese for those that donte have a JOB.
Yours.
Boy, non-certificate. Unemployed, formerly a labourer.

The older folk must re-tyre at a younger age ie 60, 61, and create more jobs for the young.
Boy, non-certificate. Labourer on experience scheme.

Well! Some jobs you go for your to young other's they want school leaver's And others youve no exspereance. I think they should pay off the Maried Women that's got husbands working to Make Room for school leavers. or for the summer season get a way take a friend and work at some Holliday Camp's, I am waiting on word back, I am not eighteen yet but if youve got to lie to get into a job why not alot of people get into job's that way. Any way theres no job's here.
Girl, non-certificate. Unemployed.

I had to stay on at school for 3 months after my sixteenth birthday and I felt that these 3 months were a waste of time as we were'nt really learning anything. Due to the fact of these 3 months I had to refuse a very good job in an office in a large factory because the School would not allow me to leave. I have no difficulties in my present job and I like my work very much.
1) Bring the retirement age for men down to 60 years
2) Bring the retirement age for women down to 55 years

3) Reduce the working week to at least 35
hours
4) Curb overtime
5) Employers should take on more school
leavers
   instead of advertiser for skilled worker and
   train them thereselves.
(1–5 would enable more jobs for young people).
   Girl. O grades, no A–C awards. Office junior.

I havent really found anything difficult at work.
I am in a Training College at work with
Shipbuilders and once I had settled in and got
to know the people I was working with it was
just like school really only we concentrate on
joinery. My company has recently let 196
people use our facilities in our college with the
government paying them. I think this is good
because they will be able to learn welding,
burning, plating, etc. So this could help them
get a permanent job.
   *Boy. O grades, no A–C awards. Apprentice
   joiner.*

When I left school, I did not know what type of
work I would like to do. My dad said I was
quite good working with tools. After I had a
talk with him I decided to try for a motor
mechanic's Job. My dad took me around several
garages and was fortunate to get an apprentice
ship.
I suggest to help young people leaving school at
16 should be giving the oppertunity to vist
various types of industry This would help them
decide what type of job to look for.
I suggest that large factories, should take more
apprentives. eg. My dads factory employes
about 2500 workers and only 12 apprentices
each year. I think that this firm could take at
least *36* apprentices, *AND* at the end off the
apprentice ship if there is no work, at least they
have been trained in a craftsman's job.
   Boy, non-certificate. Apprentice mechanic.

Work is not so easily found as everyone seems
to think. It takes time, time which one cannot
afford to waste. And the work you get maybe
harder than expected which means more effort
is required to keep on working there. I think a
new more improved system should be devised
to supply school leavers and job-hunters with a
job to suit there ability. One like what I sat to
get into Her Majesty's Armed Forces. I thought
I would get into the regiment I wanted but
instead because I had not enough marks in the
test I was put into a different one altogether.
I think that a system like that would be ideal
because then an employer who wanted high
standards got the pick of the high passes and
other employers got the rest.

Many units using this method should be put
throughout the country and in schools to help
people find the job they are suited to best of all.
   *Boy, non-certificate. On a work experience
   scheme.*

I think to make it easier for young school
leavers to obtain work, it to make more jobs
available by trying to build more Factorys,
Industries etc.
   Girl, non-certificate. Office worker.

'. . . because staggering numbers of unemployed'
views on special schemes for unemployed young people

I think there should be more work or schemes
for school leavers because of the staggering
numbers of unemployed. When you are out of
work for a long period you would probably get
very deppessed and soon give up looking. I am
on the Government Training Scheme for six
months and I have to sit a test for a proper
Apprenticeship as an Electrician. I am also very
confident I will pass my test.
   Boy, non-certificate. Electrician.

The only thing I liked about school was my 1st
2nd and 3rd years, after that school was just a
boar. Well when in your 4th year you use to
get treated like a 1st year pupil and all you kept
saying was 'I wish i were working'. I find
nothing difficult at my work. There should be
more factories which should start school leavers
write away or they should be doing some-thing
for the gover-ment and getting payed from the
gover-ment. The gover-ment should be doing
more than they are doing at present to find jobs
for school leavers. And not putting them on the
dole.
   Boy, non-certificate. Working in a distillery.

Since I have started working I have not really
had any difficulties as the firm I work with is
very good. I live near where I work and also the
people I work with are very nice and always
eager to help with any necessary training. When
looking for a job the only thing that caused me
some difficulty was the fact that I had failed my
'O' grade exams. But apart from that I had no
real difficulties, considering I was only
unemployed for three weeks. In order to help
young people leaving school I think that every

company should have someone working in every branch under the job creation scheme. There is a lot of work people can learn under these trial schemes especially in office work and dealing with the public as there is a lot of experience to be gained. There is another point I would like to raise that is I feel that there are so many people who leave school and just don't care, they leave school and just 'sign-on' at the unemployment agency weekly. I personally, think there are more jobs than some people claim, because I feel that if people really put there minds to obtaining a job they will if they just keep on trying.

Girl, non-certificate. Clerkess.

I have not got much to say for myself. To make jobs better for school leavers I think employers should take them on under the work experience Programme as it can help, I finish work experience on the 24th August and I am now looking for a job, with the advantage that I can now say to the employers that I have had experience in office work or any other work. Sometimes I would like to go back to school and take different subjects because I would like a job where I met new people, the place had a good atmosphere, I travel some places. There is really not much to say except that I would like to see more jobs for young school leavers.

Girl, non-certificate. Left her first (unknown) job because 'there was no prospects for me'. On a work experience scheme as an office junior.

I enjoyed school a lot because you had a lot of friends there, and through time you really got to know the teachers, who helped any time they could. Then the time came to look for a job, which was very difficult, but all there was left was just to keep on trying until something came along. Finally I got started in a short industrial course, which I got through the careers office. Just now there seems to be a lot of these government training schemes, now these scheme's would be enjoyable for the unemployed just now, but personally I think they should be extended for an extra year or so, because I was just beginning to get used to the machinery and starting to enjoy myself when the course was just about folded up. I certainly enjoyed the course and would still like to get back into the engineering trade.

Boy, non-certificate. Clothes shop assistant.

When I started looking it was terrible every job I applied for they said I had no experience so when I got the chance of a work experience I jumped to it. Now when I leave it I will have experience and a referance. So there should be a work experience course for every school leaver that should give them the chance that I got. about school it was okay but for the last year I got work that I done in 2nd year.

Boy, O grades, no A–C awards. On a work experience scheme as a farm worker.

I think the Goverments Work Experience Programme is really a good thing. It gave me lots of experience and I met lots of different people.
At first I didn't really fancy the idea of working on it, but am very glad I did and it will help me greatly in finding a perminant job.
Looking back to the time when I was unemployed I realise why I didn't get a job, the lack of experience.

Girl. O grades, no A–C awards. On a work experience scheme as an office junior.

I have not found it too difficult to find a job, but I have been on social security twice.
I think that there should be more opportunities for young people, and more help to find jobs. These schemes which are now open to young people are very good, it keeps them from social security and gives them a chance to get more experience at working.

Girl, non-certificate. On a work experience scheme as a secretary.

I am glad I was taken into Job creation scheme [work experience] I think I learned a lot about woodwork and I am grateful that they got me a Job in a boat building yard if it wasnt for them I dont think I would ever have got the trade I want to learn. I have quite a good chance of getting kept on and learn my trade, I think Job creation is a good thing.

Boy. O grades, no A–C awards. On a work experience scheme at a boat yard.

I found it hard adapting to the working rules, and also when I was unemployed I was in the local job centre every week and the 'wee' cards always say 'must have experience', 'must be over such "n" such an age.' I think they have done enough to help young people by bringing the Government Youth Organisation by paying them £20.55. Okay, maybe its not much but it gives them the feeling that they are part of the everyday working world.

Boy, non-certificate. Van boy.

The job creation schemes etc does not help young people at all instead of having these schemes for six months or more they should be extended for a year course. When employers take on (WEPs) Work Experience people, they sometimes promise they might get kept on in the shop or factory. But as the time draws up the person or persons involved time is nearly up and they ask if there is a chance of a permanent job within the company they answer is normally no. there's always a catch in it somewhere. Its just cheap labour to the company or companies involved don't have to hand out large amounts of money. Some companies are too darn lazy to take on extra manpower in case say for example they take 50 people on. Maybe these people are not very good workers so they get shot of them. So they decide to bring in cheap labour which happens to be young WEPs. the companies sometimes have no intensions to keep WEPs on if they are good workers or not.

Girl, non-certificate. Assembly line worker in a food processing factory during her work experience scheme. Unemployed.

Dear MADAM,
I have no complant about scool But Job creachon is just cheep labour I work 40 hr week for £20-55 as I am the youngst I get the heve end of the stick I was under the imppress I would be cookine But all I Do is wash dishes. Some tranin IM gittin.
Yours anoyed.

Girl, non-certificate. On a work experience scheme.

I am nearly 17 yrs old, and now after the last job I was in finished it seems even harder to get an other one, especially with more school leavers leaving school at Christmas.
Sometimes you do feel that you wish you were back at school with no responsibilities or worries about getting a job. These government backed schemes are a good thing but being only temporary you are just back to square one. so I think the the government should concentrate on getting permanent jobs for school leavers.

Boy. O grades, no A–C awards. Unemployed. Previously on a work experience scheme.

More should be done for unemployed off all ages. Work expeirence should be stopped as you are just getting into the way of working when you are shoved back on the dole heap. It cost the employers nothing as the goverment pays the wages the employers then turn round and employ someone else. Until their time is up. Personally speaking this pamphlet is also a waste of time as it will most likely be put back at the back off a shelf and forgotten.
sincerely

Boy, non-certificate. Left his first job in the Armed Forces because 'too much discipline'. Unemployed. Left a work experience scheme before it was due to finish.

About this job creation if you get a job in the nearest town by the time you pay your bus fares you have not got very much left for yourself and most of them just take you for a pure *skivy* and I don't think it is a good scheme.

Girl, non-certificate. Unemployed. Worked as a hotel cleaner on a work experience scheme.

When I left school my parents freinds & relitives were the only ones who helped me to get a job When I went to the Careers office and they got me a work experiance but in six monthes I was back in the streets again I think that if they cant find you a permanent job they should not raise your hopes but there should be more help for young people.

Girl, non-certificate. Her first job was as a packer; later on a work experience scheme she did similar work. Works in a shop.

Nothing is difficult at work but when looking for work I think it is very hard to find a good job. Well the work experience and job creation are good things but I think they should pay more because young people get nearly as much on the brew instead of working like that they only get a few pounds more and they do nothing for it. I think the pay is silly the pay is £20.55 you get £14.75 on the brew so who wants to work for a few pounds extra would you unless bored.

Boy, non-certificate. On a work experience scheme as a gardener.

I don't like working in the Job Scheme put out by the govermet because I got just as much on the Brew when I just sign a piece of paper so when I leave when my time is up I woun't take another job unless it's full-time. Thank you, I only glad that I could help you.

Boy, non-certificate. On a work experience scheme as a store and kitchen worker.

I find it difficult to consintrate on my work everything is just a mad rush the joiners dont spend much time showing you anything because of this bonus scheme I think it is ridiculous in another ten year there will not be very many craftsmen left. I think this job creation think should be stopped it is just cheap labour take this for instance I was working on an outside job on a roof we were out two days my and my journy men wene the gafer came out and replaced me with one of these job creation boys I was very cut about the whole thing that I complained to my charge hand who said that it costs to put me out on a job wether it disent cost them a penny for the job creation boy ever since I havent learned much outside work since he started. So I wonder should I chuck my job and start on a job creation scheme? Well it only lasts for 6 months but Ill learn more in that 6 months rather than stuck in the workshop.

Boy, non-certificate. Assembly line worker in a factory before becoming an apprentice joiner because 'I was offered an apprenticeship wich I jumped at'.

'Scrap O levels and make everything equal'
opposition to job selection based on certificates

I found difficulty in finding work because I had no O' grades and most of the jobs were looking for people with them. Scrap O levels and make everything equal.

Boy, non-certificate. Building labourer.

I liked school because it was good fun. And I know that it is very hard to find a job for young people with no *Qualifications—O'Grade ect.* Teachers think they know every thing about youths today but they dont that's one problem about adults today if you want to know more of my oppinion please let me know.

Boy, non-certificate. Seaman.

I liked maths and arithmetic at school, the only thing I didn't like and that was physical education. I never sat any O levels as I left school before I could sit them. I wish I could sit them now and get a merchandising course but I don't know how to go about it. The things I found difficult when looking for work was that they were looking for people with O levels, and you were either too young or too old for jobs I tried for, I think there should be more training schemes and that they should get a wee bit more money as it isn't really fair they do the exact same work as a normal person and get paid less.

Girl, non-certificate. Shop assistant.

I disliked school because of the strictness of it. Also whats the point of listing to youre guidance teacher and carrers officer telling you about the different jobs you want, when you know the first chance of a job comes, youre just going to take it and not bother what it is because jobs are so hard to come by if you havent got o' grades. When I was at school six weeks before we left we got out of school 2½ days a week to look for jobs around the local

firms. This is how I got my job but it wasnt what I wanted I knew that I wouldnt get the job I wanted so I just took it. To help young people get a job you should scrap the o level system give them a equal chance with the people that might be brainner than them when leaving school just give them a certificate saying they completed their education satasfactory.

Boy, non-certificate. Apprentice bricklayer.

I am 17 years old with no O levels the only thing I wish is to have stayed on to sit my O levels as it would help me if I wanted another job, I liked most of my subjects at school except English as I did not find the teacher very good at teaching. When looking for work I have found it difficult as employers are looking for people with O levels before those who have none. To help yong people who are looking for work I think employer's should be spoken to asking them to give youngsters at least 6 weeks trial and train them, as I think yongster's could learn a trade even without O levels if taught correctly.

Girl, non-certificate. Clothes machinist.

I liked school, I liked playing at all sports especialy Rugby football and Running, I also liked cooking and sewing, because it was something diffrent all the time you made some interesting things at sewing, and it also lernt you to do your own clothes and cook your own meals. I found that not sitting my exames and having no o levels that was my bigest disadvantage. I think that if one person wants to do A job he would like, to do he should have more time at the subjects that would help him to get the job that he wants and then I think they would try a lot harder, to get the job they wanted.

Boy, non-certificate. Formerly a shop assistant. Miner.

Im very keen to be a Painter and decorator but my chances are next to none because Ive got no O LEVELS my own opinion I don't really think you need O LEVELS to be a tradesman as it never happened in days gone by.

Boy, non-certificate. Worked as a painter and decorator on a short industrial course for unemployed young people. Unemployed.

I don't find anything very difficult in my work as there is nothing difficult in selling clothes. The most difficult thing in trying to find a job was the amount of people that were all going for the one job. I think the best thing to help young people looking for jobs is to do away with O levels. Just because somebody has got more O levels than you does not mean to say

that he is a better worker than you.
Boy. O grades, no A–C awards. Shop assistant.

When you have no O' levels, you have no other alternative but factory work.
Girl, non-certificate. Clothes machinist.

I would just like to say that I the the employment system is wrong because to get a good job these days you have to have O'levels. I have always wanted to be an electrician and I would make a very good electrician as it is something that is natural to me I can pick it up very easily but I have never been given a chance to prove that is is what I am very good at. I am now just about 17½ years old and if I do not get a chance in the very near future I will never get a chance because I am just about to old for an apprenticeship. maybe you can HELP ME!
Boy, non-certificate. Electrical insulation fitter; formerly apprentice butcher.

I don't think my last year at school was worthwhile at all as we didnt really learn anything new unless we decided to sit O' levels. I decided against O' levels after I was told I had the ability to pass them because I think if you try hard enough you can get a good enough job without them. I proved myself right on this point by landing a good job in a Bank Printing Dept. I enjoy this Job very much and although I spent three months looking for a job I'm glad I didnt end up in a dead-end job in a shop or factory. When I was unemployed it was very disheartening going after one job with about ten other applicants but Im convinced that if you keep on trying you must succede in the end.
Boy, non-certificate. Printing machine operator.

I think most of the jobs should do away with the young people having to have O level.
Boy, non-certificate. Shop assistant.

I left school early to look after my young sister as my mum was ill so I lost half a term but I dont think that it would have made any difference to what I already was.
I would have liked to have got O levels but when I got into my last year I thought they would'nt have been any use as I thought I could get a well paid job without them. But I've tried hard to get a job with no luck and now wish that I had stayed on at school.
Girl, non-certificate. Unemployed.

I diden't attend school reguarly because in my last year the school dident give us any thing of intrest, I was in one of the lower classes and we dident get O level work. I myself think that all classes should be made the same because if you are in the lower classes you lose all intrest in school. I think that when someone like myself leaves school it is hard to find a job because every where you go they want expericince. Every young person looking for work after leaving school should be given the same chance as anyone alse whether they have O grades or not.
Girl, non-certificate. Shop assistant.

I had two years of part time education which didn't help matters when looking for work. I liked the last years at school because we didn't get much lessons, the teachers could have helped by telling us about jobs and how to apply for them. I have been a milk boy up until Jan. this year, and I've been looking for work every where since then, most jobs need O levels and there is so much boys out of work, what chance is there.
Boy, non-certificate. Unemployed.

To much emphasis put on certificates instead of personalities.
I would like to see employers more willing to give young people a chance to *prove* their worth instead of going by certificates. I was fortunate this was done in my case. But my sister who is nearly twenty and still at college because she did not quite have enough qualifications for her desired career of nursing in my oppinon it is not acedemic genuse who make the best nurses. I enjoy my work and there is oppertunity to better myself hence the reason I am going to night school for typing. This was the one subject I was interested but was refused a commercial course at school and after thant I had no interest whatso ever in school. I am sure this happens to many young people. School is dull if you are unable to take the subjects you are interested in, and I am thankful I have been given the chance to make something of my life before it was too late.
Girl, non-certificate. Mailing clerkess. Taking an O grade in typing at F.E. college.

My name is _____, I am seventeen years old and attended _____ Secondary School for 3½ years up until 23 December 1977.
At School I dont think we were told enough of the difficulties in finding a job, also I think once you are put in non O'grade subjects, teachers just dont seem to bother with you, like they should do. They leave you sitting around while they concentrate on the O'grade pupils.
I realise now I would have been better to sit my O'Levels, as most jobs look for qualifications. As I was unemployed for 1 year, I feel it's because I had no qualifications.

I think young people should be told the
difficulties in finding work. Also I think Pupils
should see a Careers Office before leaving
school, As I havn't seen anyone about this. Also
I think the 'Job Creation Scheme' should be
more publicised as many dont know a thing
about it. I hope this information helps your
Survey for Teenagers.
Girl, non-certificate. Trainee cook.

I liked THE DINNERS. I didn't like the fact
that because there is a group of us on NON
CERTIFACATE courses it didn't matter that
we got a careers teacher for arithmatic or a
modern studies teacher for secratarial studies or
any kind of teacher for music.
Everything is difficult at first untill your taught
and get into the way of things and then you
wonder they you couldn't do it in the first
place.
Fortunately. I never had any difficulty in
getting a job.
Get rid of this need for O' levels when going
for a job. I think if your set on doing a certain
job the employer should be willing to train you
and if you are willing to learn you should be
able to handle it. If not you couldn't have
wanted the job that much in the first place.
Girl, non-certificate. Apprentice hairdresser.

Sorry to say I was not very keen on school.
Teachers were not to blame I was just incapable
of learning.
Regards out of work I think some firms could
give young people a chance without A or O
levels as I myself can learn quick when shown
how to do a job. I dont think at the moment
there is an answer to your last question Britains
Industries are bad all over. They say men now
may retire at 60. Perhaps it will give young
boys a chance then.
Boy, non-certificate. Unemployed for 10 months.

I was in a remedial class at school. The
Teachers I had were helpful to me and I got on
well with most of them.
The most difficult part of finding a job is that I
have no certificates to show employers and as I
have not got much confidense I feel at a
disadvantage. I am willing to work and as my
school record shows I am a good time keeper,
and had an excellent attendance record yet I
have nothing in writing to prove this.
I am sorry I have no ideas on what should be
done to help young people find a job, but I feel
in my sort of case that more help could be
given.
Girl, non-certificate. Unemployed.

CHAPTER EIGHT

'BRIGHT PEOPLE GET ON FINE WITHOUT HELP'

Views from the certificate side

Although I realise what the teacher has to cope with, each teacher could be more concerned with the pupil rather than the pupils attainments, without detracting from what she teaches or from what is being learned. Most of our teachers concentrated on bright pupils, encouraging them which is wrong because bright people get on fine without help, while the less able pupils get moved into, a lower non-certificate class and the attitude was, 'we only have to put up with them until they reach S.L.A., we'll just keep them occupied until then,' with no care about preparing them for life outside school in any way.

Girl, Highers*. Studying social sciences at university.

1) In my school, and many others I believe, there are two different 'classes' of pupils. Pupils who hardly need teaching as they practically live by swotting to please teacher and get way ahead of teachers schedule. This creates an impression on the class teachers, and the teachers respond with great enthusiasm for the pupil. Now the pupil is more than likely right by what he or she is doing, and working very hard, but the '2nd class' of pupils is people like myself, who like to get on well at school but cant be bothered with work at home, (which to me is absolutely unnecessary, as I think schoolchildren do enough at school without doing more in our own time), and the intellectual pupil, who shows off his outstanding 'I.Q.' to all other 'not so bright' pupils.

The point I am making is, SOME teachers are the main reason why pupils are embarrased to answer questions in class in case they are quietly laughed at by the 'Intellectuals', and also to work for future exams, (I will write later on, on this page about my plight on this subject). Most teachers love attending to, and helping the 'brainy' pupil and can't be really bothered with the ones that need more help, although the teachers will testify to the exact opposite. The answer to your question therefore, is I, and many others, were treated like complete outcasts in school. The more school went on, the more the teachers made it unbearable for you, as this is shown in the classes I was in. This 'slump' from 1st year in my case, was due to being sick and tired of the treatment, and attitude of teachers towards you, and this resulted in my own 'slump' in attitude towards my own work, and confidence in doing so.

2) Referring to questions on EXAMS, I only sat 2, but in fact was supposed to sit four, English and Arithmetic, which I sat, and Geography and History which I didn't owing to reasons which I have stated in the last point, (No. 1). I never bothered to attend 2 exams because I lost all confidence in myself leading up to the exams because of teachers continually saying things like, 'You'll never do', 'usless', 'thick', and other words, never uttered to an intellectual. Personally I think most exams are useless, because most pupils end up with jobs that had nothing to do with the things they were taught at school.

3) Too many teachers, after being asked a question, say 'If you don't know that, you'll never pass the exam. Go to the library and find out'. Surely they are getting paid to answer even the most simplest of questions?

I have enjoyed doing this survey and enjoyed to express my views at last, on the scanalous condition of teaching standards in schools today. If there are any more questions you would like to ask, please do, as I would only be too willing to help out.

Boy, O grades. * Miner.

* 'Highers' means attempted or passed at least one SCE H grade. As an abbreviated description in this final chapter, 'O grades' means that at least one award in the range A-C had been achieved in the SCE O grade examination.

The purpose of the remaining sections is twofold. First, they provide a second and independent perspective on the writings of the non-certificate leavers. What follows has been written exclusively by leavers who achieved some SCE certification; that is, they had gained at least one SCE O grade subject at A–C and usually many more than this. The small selection reproduced here indicates an awareness of the plight of the 'forgotten' children among those pupils whom the schools had remembered. Second, the selection indicates that many of the issues about which non-certificate leavers wrote with such feeling either extended to, or had their counterpart among, the experiences of pupils on certificate courses. For example the hierarchy of academic esteem which non-certificate pupils had experienced overwhelmingly in terms of two classes of pupil, turns out in some of the accounts here to consist in fact of several classes; 'middle of the road' pupils, or pupils not interested in university, could also feel disregarded. Or they could feel that well-meaning curricular decisions had been taken on their behalf the implications of which they nevertheless resented: 'When deciding our subjects for 3rd year it was all accepted that 2A should take latin, physics, chemistry etc. They didn't think what we might want to do after leaving school. . . It was expected that a large majority of our class should go to University'.

Thus the question of the utility of the curriculum, and of its relevance, interest and importance also preoccupied many of the academically more able school leavers. They had, moreover, also to contend with the pressures of passing the public examinations from which non-certificate pupils were excluded, the examinations that 'can make or break you'. One of those whom examinations 'made', a medical student, writes of the success of his school in achieving high pass rates in the certificate examinations through the use of 'teaching methods firmly entrenched in the 19th Century'. With the exception of one subject (Biology) his conclusion is 'School-work largely, if not wholly, irrelevant to present course of study. Subject matter taught in school is highly restrictive and geared towards the passing of the out-dated and predictable SCE certificate examinations'. The correspondence between this and the conclusions of many of the non-certificate leavers is disconcerting.

And so too is the conclusion of another university student: '. . . My main complaint was that we were treated badly by teachers. I do not mean physically badly (although certain teachers were guilty of physical malpractice eg belting on wrists, adding force to the belting by jumping off chairs!!). We were treated wrongly. If we were treated in senior years at school as responsible human beings able to decide what is best for us, the school would have found discipline much easier to maintain. As it was any small step out of line resulted in a reaction by staff that was ridiculously out of proportion to the crime commited. If relations and understanding between staff could be improved in the school it would, without a doubt, lead to a more efficient, enjoyable and easier to work system. Until this is obtained anarchy will rule, future generations will suffer and school will remain in the eyes of children a place of hatred, defiance and above all sheer frustration'.

It is also the case, however, that a large majority of Highers and O grade children enjoyed their last year of school (Appendix, Table 3) and that a majority of them thought it worthwhile (Appendix, Table 2). (The surveys do not record what Highers pupils thought about their fourth year at school, the year in which the majority of O grade presentations are made, and the final year, of course, for most of the non-certificate pupils). As Table 1 of the Appendix reminds us, over half the age group left school with an A–C award in the SCE O grade, or with something better.

But just under half left either with no SCE awards or with awards only at the D or E grade, and over a third were never presented for an SCE examination. We may remind ourselves in conclusion that a majority of these non-certificate leavers had not enjoyed their last year at school and a larger majority did not think it had been worthwhile. Many faced difficulties in finding work and a substantial minority experienced lengthy unemployment. Around a third wished they could read and write better and two thirds wished they were better at arithmetic. About a quarter had truanted for days or weeks at a time during their final year and over half had been belted quite often or often during their time at secondary school. Around seven out of ten had no regrets that they left school when they did.

From about 1982 onwards, the children of the leavers whose accounts we have been reading will themselves be starting full-time education.

'If you were above average in our school you took Latin, Physics and Chemistry'
curriculum, academic and non-academic

When I look back to when I was at school. I feel we were influenced by how clever or bright we were. In the first year we were divided into any class not depending on our IQ or intelligence from our primary schools. Though our marks in Exam's in 1st year, we put together and from there we were put in classes for 2nd year. The best marks being class 2A. I for one was in class 2A, and we were all called the 'brainy lot'. When deciding our subjects for 3rd year it was all accepted that 2A should take latin, physics, chemistry etc. They didn't think what we might want to do after leaving school and these subjects might not help us. It was expected that a large majority of our class should go to University.

I personally had no wish to go to University and knew that I would like to nurse or train to become a secretary. I always remember some teachers shocked that I was the only one in my class not taking physics and chemistry, but taking secretarial studies and biology. Now in 1979, I have started my nursing training and I have a friend in sixth year taking a crash course in secretarial studies, after trying her physics and chemistry and deciding is was not for her. I found we were never advised about our future at all. If you were above average in our school you took Latin, Physics and Chemistry if you were below average, like most girls took Food and Nutrition. Maybe I was influenced by my older brothers who are clever and attended University. Both coming out with degrees. My older brother has been looking for a job for 2 years now while he works in the job creation scheme. My parents are very disheartened about them both. As my other brother has got a job but with no future being sought. My parents put them both through University, while I came straight out of school and into Nursing and getting more out of it than my brothers have got from going to University. Generally I feel the whole educational running is wrong, and we are never advised rightly. Or given the right information. I was lucky, I knew what I wanted to do and mostly found out myself and from my parents what I needed for my Nursing career.

Girl, Highers. Student nurse.

School could be greatly improved if the teachers took a personal interest in the pupils, and gave positive statements about queries concerning colleges etc. I think that in my school teachers had no interest in 'middle of the road' pupils and where only interested in pupils that were going to universities. The course that finished up in was constrived by no help from guidance teachers, teachers etc.
Any advice I would give to a secondary pupil would be to leave school after 4th year and do highers at a college.

Girl, Highers. Taking a full-time course in commercial studies at F.E. college.

Starting a new job was like starting from scratch, I feel the only useful thing I learned at school was how to change a plug. Too much emphasis was put on going to university at my school, when the careers teacher discovered I did not want to go to university, or college, he never gave me a second thought, not even some advice about how to start looking for a suitable job. I had to write away and find out for myself what jobs were available. This I could not have done had I not relatives working in the field which I entered.

Girl, Highers. Applied to university, but working as a computer operator.

I found that in the school I attended _____ teachers were willing to help if you approached them. But help was only given to everyone at certain times of the year e.g. before leaving school etc. I had 2 meetings with the careers officer while at school; neither of them had I mentioned any wish to teach, so they were, in retrospect, rather pointless. There was an attempt made to introduce a guidance teacher to the school, but this had to be stopped because so few people were taking advantage of it. One thing I regret about my secondary education is the fact that I was in a class with others who were labelled as 'academic pupils', with the result that in my second year, whilst others were given secretarial studies or food and nutrition, I was given German. I then felt that because I had started the subject, I may as well carry it on. But although it has not been any great help with my career, it has not hindered it any. All in all I feel any help I did receive were very fragmented and I think more help should be given to pupils further down the secondary school, because it is then that they have to choose subjects—which is tantamount to choosing their career. I think that it must be difficult for a second year pupil who has no idea what they want to do later to choose subjects for study now. Perhaps it would be better for someone who has no idea what they

want to do should choose as varied a timetable
of subjects as possible, because then they won't
be disappointed when then decide on their
career and find they don't have the
qualifications to follow it. In some subjects you
can take a higher without sitting the 'O' Grade,
so that, on reaching 5th year (3 years after their
initial choice of subjects) they will have a
clearer idea on what they want to do, and can
drop subjects and take new ones accordingly. I
do realise that this might not work in all cases,
but it could help some people. I certainly think
its better than taking say three languages and
then finding you want to do physiotherapy of
something else requiring scientific
qualifications.

Girl, Highers. Primary student teacher.

I think it is very sad that so little time is spent
on subjects relevant to everyday life. After
second year all the pupils are automatically
ushered into a studying subjects such as French,
Physics, chemistry and such like. I think all
pupils should receive more guidance at second
year as this is a very important time and the
choice will affect their whole career. In my
second year when I was choosing subjects the
guidance staff were extremely unhelpful. They
were merely trying to hurry up and get the
forms filled in. The only help I received was
from my parents and family.
Also, pupils who are not likely to partake in
further education who are not interested in
sitting O'levels and such like should be given
opportunities to study practical subjects such as
home Economics, Dressmaking, health
Education. First Aid lessons should be
compulsory in all schools and other subjects
which are basic to everyday life eg hygiene,
nutrition.
In conclusion, the educational system appears to
be geared towards catering for those pupils
interested in further education. Other pupils
don't appear to get any advantages from going
to school.

*Girl, Highers. Taking a degree course in
nursing studies.*

School is still geared to the academically
minded child and some teachers think the rest
are all nit-wits! The chosen few are still catered
for. Sometimes they forget that there is a big
world outside the school with all kinds of work
in it.

Boy, O grades. Apprentice engineer.

'. . . . Interesting . . . (but) irrelevant'
the relevance of the curriculum

Although the courses at school were made as
interesting as they could be I found that they
were often irrelevant to life when I left school. I
also have forgotten a great deal that I have
learned in particular French and German
because I have had no reason to speak or read
the languages. The only main benefits my four
highers and 8 'O' grades have been to me is in
getting a higher rate of pay for having them.
The 'O' grade courses were more practical and
useful for everyday knowledge because they
were not so specialised. Higher English was also
very good because it helps in your
understanding of plays and forms etc.

Girl, Highers. Bank teller.

Actually this made me think that most of my
subjects don't really come into Banking, and
this made me think—was it worth sitting seven
O grades when English and Arithmetic would
have done. But I want to work abroad and
French and Geography and maybe Commercial
Studies will then prove vital, also I have a
grounding in these subjects which means I can
go for further education in the future.

Girl, O grades. Bank clerk.

I enjoyed most of my school life but I feel that
most of my subjects were purely geared towards
me passing an exam and was not really teaching
the subject so it would help you in a future job.
Most subjects taught at school and the way they
are taught are totally irrelevent to future work.
I admit we need basics, but then there should
be some practical work. Also, I understand the
Education Authorities have a tight budget but
they should try *not* to allow school books to
become out of date as was very common when I
was at school. Surely even up to date syllabus'
for the teachers to dictate to pupils would be
better than nothing.

Girl, Highers. Clerical officer in civil service.

I would tell a secondary pupil to make the most
of his/her schooldays and to make the most of
any teaching and to try and decide—and take
his/her time to decide—what to do with the
future before leaving school. Although most
people are dying to leave and get out of school,
I think that after a while the majority would
wish to go back if it was at all possible. I know
I do.

I do not agree that in your 5th and 6th yr you should be made to take a certain amount of subjects. I think that you should be encouraged more to study the subject which will be relevant to your future career, and, if the shortage of staff or classroom facilities are the problem, then the authorities should let you use the time for private study into the relevant subjects. After all it is your future career that is at stake.
Girl, Highers. Taking a course in printing design in F.E. college.

I feel that pupils should choose a few subjects (two or three) excl. English (it should be compulsory) at an earlier stage of education and specialize in these subjects. Personally I feel I had to wide a range of subjects to absorb them all. Whereas if I had concentrated on 2 or 3 subjects (excl. English) I could have passed these subjects in less time and taken them at advanced level earlier. As it was I feel I wasted a lot of time studying for subjects of no use to me. So rather than filling timetables with subjects you have no interest in pupils should be able to concentrate on subjects related to one and other. To do so I realize that pupils would have to have an idea of what kind of employment they wish to enter. Personally I knew I would enter into some sort of administration as I not work with my hands. I must say most pupils have a rough idea as I did, eg. Technical, Commercial etc.
Boy, Highers. Works for H.M. Customs and Excise.

If I was to start my school curriculum again practical subjects would be the order of the day ie. Secretarial Studies, Accounting This unfortunately is only something you realise *after* the event, no matter how much good advice was available, which it was. At the end of the day the pupil makes *his* choice come hell or high water and for better or worse. I am happy with my time spent in the senior school. Any mistakes are my own.
Boy, Highers. Trainee administrator.

At school I learned very very little about people living in hard conditions etc. I think although this can be learned from out of school conditions, it would be advisable to have social workers etc to talk in schools for the benefit of everyone. When I came to the job I am in now I knew little about the needs of disturbed children or their circumstances. Six months in this kind of work has made a great impact on me. The aspects of my schooling were that we were all treated as individuals. We had many different interesting school groups, (discussion groups etc) at which lots could be learned, and

throughout the years of my schooling lots of trips, conferences, meetings and out of door facilities were made use of to the benefit of each and everyone.
Girl, Highers. Assistant housemother.

A) in addition to, or instead of, the teaching of physical education, I feel more benefit could be attained from various forms of health exercises and meditation such as yoga.
B) Schools should be geared towards teaching pupils to be adults through moral and social sciences. If a person wants academic education, this should be their individual choice, and taken after school. In other words, a system similar to North American ones.
C) I would like to see better facilities for Art, Music, Drama etc, in Music, instead of singing or hearing records, instrument instruction should be readily available.
Boy, Highers. Studying computing science at university.

I found that the majority of subjects I did at school were worthwhile in that either they are useful at University or from a general, knowledge point of view. An example is secretarial, because although I am never likely to be a secretary the ability to be able to type etc is very useful and also the knowledge of how to set out letters properly and so forth is useful. I would not reccomend anyone to leave school for University at the end of Fivth Year as I think the majority of people of that age are not mature enough to cope with the new-found academic freedom. In this light the CSYS courses relevant to the university course are very useful in that you tend not to get thrown in at the deep end when you do get to University. To anybody at school I would say that in Fivth Year they should try to get as many Highers as possible and if they have no idea of what work/further education they want to do they should try to cover as wide a band of subjects as possible so that as many courses of action as possible are left open.
With jobs being so difficult to get at present Highers are essential because an employer will usually pick and choose on the strength of exam marks and the interview, and if you have a good selection of Highers then that is you half-way there. There is no point in studying obscure and sociologically 'trendy' subjects such as leisure education or social education because employers are not interested in wether you can meaningfully occupy your leisure time but can you do you job efficiently. Wether or not you agree with this attitude is irelevant. It is the attitute which exists and all you can do, from a pupils point of view, is accept it. There is no

point in producing socially aware people if you can't get a job because social awareness does not buy food and houses.

On the subject of Sixth Year, I think that Sixth Year is what you make it. You have to put something in to get something out. You should be there for a reason and not just because it is the only thing to do. You should not expect to spoon fed with happiness in Sixth Year. As in life, happiness or enjoyment usually has to be created, to have something, ie work, put into it. I would be very interested to hear from you about the results and conclusions you draw from your survey some time in the future.

Boy, Highers. Studying electrical engineering at university.

Dear Sir, Madame,

I think that some of the Lessons I took at School Helped me to find a Job. The Subjects like Maths, Arithmetic, Physics, Chemistry helped me in my job but some of the other subjects I was forced too take in 1st and second year used up a lot of the time that could have been put to improving your chance's at getting an 'O' level in the subjects which would help in finding a job. These subjects like Latin and cooking were forced upon you and unless you were going to take a job as a Roman cook would be no use to you in later life. If the programme of lessons had been changed so that the boys had say lessons on car maintenance then they would have some knowledge that they could use in later life.

Concerning what was good about School I think the clubs organised by a lot of the teachers in my school helped to help the pupils interested in attending school and it gave them a chance to let off steam and this meant they where able to concentrate more on their exams because they where more relaxed.

Boy, O grades. Apprentice electrical engineer.

I found that at school we were only taught to pass exams, which was usually to keep up the standard of the school We were not educated about life. I feel that other subjects should be taught e.g. law and how it works. Also more stress should be put on social studies and especially for 4th year upwards health education.

I discovered in my school life that I went to, listened to and learned more from teachers who had worked outside the education circle.

Perhaps it was coincidence.

Boy, Highers. Clerk.

Myself, and three friends, started to do lighting for school productions in our fourth year.

We also organised and ran school disco's for the junior school. Both these activities were extended into our fifth year, which made it most enjoyable for us, as well as being rewarding. Rewarding in the sense that a certain amount of theory in the classroom could be made more clear through these activities (Physics Classroom) ie motors, pulleys, resistance etc. Also, of course, it was fun to do and was appreciated by the audiences and teachers, at these productions.

Boy, Highers. Cashier.

A lot more careers advice should Be given. For example a lot more about the basic things that happen when you start to work. Where to get you insurance card why you pay tax, what is the insurance number for. What do you do if you start your job and you are ill. How to find out more about your job.

Girl, O grades. Shop assistant.

As a first year University student I have experienced the change-over from school to Uni and it is not an easy one. I feel there must be some scheme introduced into schools which prepare people better for whatever lies ahead e.g. the case of university students I feel that when the highers finish, those who intend to, and would appear to be able to, go to University should have the opportunity of attending a short course at the University they are most interested in, at which they would be introduced to the methods of study and the contents of the courses they are interested in. They could even be told about suitable books which would help them to get into the course better. I feel this idea would greatly reduce the number of people who are sickened by the completely different set-up and greater work-rate at Uni, and would perhaps stop the great waste of money and time spent on putting students in University who then find out Uni doesn't suit them.

Boy, Highers. Studying science at university.

Non-academic people like myself feel like second class citizens at school and could do with more help with reading in the primary. We always had very large classes in primary and junior school and maybe teachers had no time to spare for the less able, slow pupils and poor readers. However I'm reluctant to read, only reading newspapers. Now that I'm 17 I feel I would like a lot more further education on social, environmental, religious, world affairs, community, etc from experienced lecturers, also more of these at school. At school all is geared to passing exams. Could more time be given to character building.

Boy, O grades. Apprentice plasterer.

Since leaving School I find that maybe just 3 of the subjects are useful to me, and they are English, Arithmetic and Secretarial Studies. The good thing about my School was the sporting side of it e.g. Hockey team etc. The parts which could be made better are making the subjects more interesting and also to take more attention of the pupils that aren't so good at the subjects and to give them more encouragement than they do. The advice I would give to someone at School would be to do their best and not worry too much because when you leave School you'll find life much more easier and happier.
    Girl, O grades. Junior clerkess.

Please read this if you can.
My O grade subjects. *Arithmetic* very badly taught, we went in to our class sat down, opened our books and were told every subject to copy down the examples he wrote on the board, as he wrote them down, but he scribbled down the examples so quick, explaining them as he went along, that we found it difficult to kept up to him, but if any of us objected to this we were sent outside for abuse, so we just had to concentrate on writing down the examples off the board as quickly as we could. Then he would tell us to do a few ourself's, most of use would have a good atempt a few would even succeed, but as the teacher never checked our books he was none-the-wiser In fourth year I ask to drop Arithmetic with a few other students, the head of maths dept, was reluctant at first, but we told him that we were getting nowhere with the subject and that it was useless continuing with the subject.
Secretarial studies In this subject the students were split into three groups because of the classes being too large. I was in the third group but I was chop and changed about so much with the rest of the student's in my class, squeezed into different groups not having time to settle down in a class of our own that most of us fell behind with the work.
History This subject I was advised to take by my year teacher but I was not a bit interested of things that had happened in the past hundreds of years ago. I really regretted taking the subject, and ask to get into another subject, but was refused.
All we did was write, write, write and write and all I got in that subject was a sore hand writing, so when it came to the O grade I stayed the half an hour and then walked out, becasue I was'nt interested and did'nt study the subject.
English All we got was reading which was mostly done by the teacher.
Art All the equipment we needed, but the teacher spoke most of the periods away, before we could get started with the art itself.
In my view my basic foundation of education came from my primary school where I was quite bright, but when I started _____ my education flopped I never got worse but I never got better either. (I have nothing to thank _____ for).
    Girl, O grades. Apprentice hairdresser.

School-work largely, if not wholly, irrelevant to present course of study. Subject matter taught at school is highly restrictive and geared towards the passing of the out-dated and predictable SCE certificate examinations. Constant review of subject and examination material is necessary at regular intervals, and viewed in the light of current trends in employment and further education courses throughout the country. The aspects of my schooling which were good were in fact the total gearing towards passing examinations. The school has a high academic reputation which it maintains by a programme designed solely to bring 'success' via high pass rates in certificate examinations. This, unfortunately, entails the use of teaching methods firmly entrenched in the 19th century. Moreover, this would seem to be by far the best method of achieving good qualifications as far the S.C.E. Board is concerned. This is indeed a sad reflection on the state of Secondary education in Scotland. My advice to a secondary pupil who is wanting to go forward to an academic course of further education would be:
a) Choose subjects carefully—there is still a strong preference in favour of the more 'traditional' subjects excercised by those in authority for admissions to universities, colleges etc. Subjects such as English, Maths, Physics, Chemistry, History, Geography and French carry more 'weight' than say, Modern Studies, Biology.
b) Think carefully before entering in to a Degree course at university. Think ahead to employment prospects and the 'worth' of the degree. Present trends appear to show that many arts degrees and social science degrees are carrying very little weight as far as job opportunities are concerned.
One final note about one of the very few subjects at school which I found to be interesting and taught in a relatively enlightened manner: Biology is a subject which is more relevant to my present course than any other. It is well taught with an excellent balance of practical and theoretical work. Despite this, however, it is not regarded as being as 'good' a qualification as a pass in Physics or Chemistry. This is borne out by my own experiences and recent correspondence in the Glasgow Herald

between secondary school teachers and pupils and University admissions committee members.
Boy, Highers. Studying medicine at university.

'School can make or break you in future life'
the relevance of certification

The advice I give is never think that school isn't important. School can make or break you in future life. I think that the teachers should put much more emphasis on the importance of O' levels & highers—*not* just in upper school (4th grade & over) but right from the first day in entering school. The feeling of suffocation I felt in sitting my prelims was almost unbearable. One minute I was happy as a lark the next I was told I was about to take the first big step of my life—I felt I was not prepared. Apart from that up to now school was the best time of my life!!
Girl, Highers. Clerical officer in the civil service.

My Advise is to get as many qualifications at school as possible even if not required for job you want. Better too many than not enough. Learn to be independent at school, don't rely on pals to make decisions for you eg choosing of 'O' levels. Don't waste too much time at school because you may regret it later.
Boy, O grades. Apprentice agricultural engineer.

I think pupils who have not got a definate future should be told more about further Education and about all the different courses. Most pupils do not realise how important O' levels are, and leave school as soon as possible. In my opinion pupils should have a goal to reach in their lives therefore they should have a definate plan of their future before they leave school. Too many young people would rather go along with friends than listen to teachers.
Girl, O grades. Taking a full-time catering course at F.E. college.

I would advise someone who is still at school,
i) Not to bother about other people leaving school ie (friends etc) THINK OF YOUR OWN FUTURE.
ii) If you have got the qualifications and knowledge that it takes to stay on at school to sit better or more exams do so now. You only get one chance.
P.S. MY PLEASURE.
Boy, O grades. Trainee storeman.

For anyone who wants to get on and get a good job Highers and O grades are a must. As most employers are looking for educated people, and they usually require them to have either O grades or highers. A good school and good teachers also help.
Girl, Highers. Civil servant.

'The rigmaroll of O grades is a farse'
the utility of certification at O grade

I would just like to say that I think the whole question of education is wrong and the whole rigmaroll of O grades is a farse. The idea that someone who has more O levels than others will get a better job is a lot of rubbish as I have seen proven since I started to work.
I am very sorry for the trouble I caused by playing truant but if they made schools more interesting I am sure the people which we are believe it or not would not do this.
Girl, O grades. Clerkess.

I would just like to make one comment, and that is that although O levels may seem very important, really in the type of job I was looking for O levels in Music, Modern Studies etc. are not very usefull but could get you a job you know nothing about, and that is why I sat Metal Work and Eng. Drawing I knew what kind of job I wanted was something to do with both of them. Some people sit O levels because they like the subject and they are not thinking about leaving school. I also think that if they started something like you stayed on at school and learned the first year of your trade their would be less unemployment.
Boy, O grades. Apprentice sheet metal worker.

The reason I gave up several O'Grade subjects which I was studying is that there are too many people with plenty O'grades who are on the brew and there are many people with no qualifications who have very good jobs or apprenticeships. O levels do not really help you to get a job as long as you have a good allround education.
Boy, O grades. Shop assistant.

'O' grades are essensial for some jobs, like electronic technicions. But as for having 'O' levels for welding or plumbing its terrible. You have seen my qualifications, I'm not saying I'm

top of the class or anything. I think I am just above average. Everytime I sit a test I usually do something wrong, (i.e. wrong calculations). In some jobs its not your head but your hands. I think employers should give you a chance. If you have 'O' levels or not (e.g. say an engineering firm started me on a trial period, my head just mite 'click', and that what I was good at.)
I think careers people should visit school, about early April, avicing you what you should do. At the moment I am unemployed not because I'm stupid but because the information service regarding jobs is terrible. I have just received leaflets from the R.A.F. If I dont get a apprenticeship or a job for that matter, I will try to join the R.A.F. My qualifications might not be good, but I'll sit an aptitude test. If that fails I'd join the army for a trade.

Boy, O grades. Unemployed since he left school.

'I do not think that the questions asked go into the subject deeply enough'
some final comments

Thank you for sending me a questionair, I am very glad to see that someone is looking into the educational system at long last, but I do not think the questions asked go into the subject deeply enough. It seems to me that you already accept most of the faults in the education of people today and that you mearly wish to question the manner in which the system is run, but having gone through school I now feel that I have wasted twelve years of *my* life, not because of the way I was taught, but what I was taught. Never in my life have I yet found a need for integral calculus, latin, french, or even pythagoras theorm, but I have occationally found a need for first aid, self defence, and a kno ledge of the law, or even how those laws are made.
Is it not about time the beurocrats in charge of education came out from behind their desks and had a look at the world. I can not remember even one word of latin, and yet I was forced to study it for two years. Would it not be a better idea to teach us something about the country we live in, its laws and regulations, or is this a deliberate plan by the beurocrats to keep us ignorant, so that one day they might rule the word?
I wonder.

Boy, Highers. Apprentice engineer.

I found my school, the most unhelpful, boring uninteresting period of my life. I was repeatedly treated as a child and was confined to a uniform and routine life. I was *never* given guidance in careers or any interesting subjects and I had to choose my own subjects and my carreer completely by myself. There were *no* adequate common-room facilities or other places of solice for the fifth yrs or sixth yrs. There were absolutely no library fascilities and even the dining room was out of bounds. Since I've went to university my life and attitudes have changed substantially for the better and I feel much more of an adult. Friends which I knew at school now seem immature and totally bored and fed up with their experiences at school—victims of the inadequate secondary schooling system in the _____. I would advice all secondary pupils to treat the school with total contempt and get stuck in to the work and get their highers and leave as soon as possible. The situation, of course, must be different at other schools and I respect this but _____ must be the most deplorable school in Scotland —a view which would be sustained by everyone at _____. As for highers and O grades, I found them totally wastefull. To get these qualifications it is possible to work a system of minimal work which a friend told me about. I tried it once and passed easily. The difference between school and university work is quite enormous and I don't think a high enough standard of work is reached in secondary schools.

Boy, Highers. Studying social science at university.

I think your questionnaire is asking all the wrong questions because education is not all about O levels and Highers. It is about learning from each other as well and also I think O levels should be completely abolished and you should be assessed by your teachers or your time at school rather than by what you did in two exams.
Finally the O level period is the dullest time at school because everything is centred around the exams and no attention is paid to enjoyment and social life.

Girl, O grades. Shop assistant.

Questionnaire unable to let me express the fact that I disliked *almost* every aspect of school & derived only the minimum necessary 'goods' from it. I derived more experience of 1970's life & 'rat race' survival from 10 months (not continuous) fulltime work in a Hotel.
Schools (mine at least) are self contradictory—they impose irrational lifestyles but claim to encourage intelligent free-thought.

—Smooth Questionnaire!
   Boy, Highers. Studying geography at university.

I think that school is not properly understood
until you have been out for several years. For
myself, I enjoyed school for what it was worth
to me in my stage of development. I got a wide
and varied education which I feel the benefit of
now. It's not so much any particular subject
which has helped me—It is more teaching you
how to apply yourself to learning and
Understanding. Every subject is just as
important in it's own Way.
It works to a System and every System has
rules, certain aspects of school could be
developed. nothing needs dramatically changed.
People never really do Punishment never done
me any harm, although enforcement of personal
opinions was quite strong.
Teaching requires an attitude of Understanding
and closeness to the pupil; I found this was
often missing and the lesson became
meaningless. For someone at school I would
say, Do what you like and what you think is
best, but always treat teachers like any other
human being and they will probably treat you
the same.
   *Boy, O grades. Working in the building
   industry.*

The subjects I studied at school have proved
relevant to my present study in that I have
continued with the same subjects. This is
because of my enjoyment in the subjects, and
satisfaction derived from them. In that it was
through my school that I 'discovered' these
subjects, I greatly appreciate my education. I
enjoyed my period of time at school in that it
not only gave an excellent education but also,
through participation in other aspects of school
life, my mental outlook was broadened. Such
participation was fundamental to my enjoyment
of school. The only advice I can offer a
secondary pupil is biased. I so enjoyed school,
and the many advantages it offerred me in the
way of friends, team activities and community
life, that it would seem stupid to leave school if
one was able to stay on.
   Girl, Highers. Studying arts at university.

Since leaving school I have looked back on it
with certain strong critisism. At school facilities
were not good enough.
Teachers generally seemed to think that we
were still young kids unable to make decisions
for ourselves. Janitors stopped us speaking to
girls in certain parts of the corridors (in fact
most parts) they seemed to think that we would
attack them or else that they would get
pregnant speaking to us. Teachers are paid to

teach subjects which no one studied eg Russian,
therefore wasting money which could be re-
allocated to areas more deserving and requiring
of it. My main complaint was that we were
treated badly by teachers. I do not mean
physically badly (although certain teachers were
guilty of physical malpractice eg belting on
wrists, adding force to belting by jumping off
chairs!!). We were treated wrongly. If we were
treated in senior years at school as responsible
human beings able to decide what is best for us,
the school would have found discipline much
easier to maintain. As it was any small step out
of line resulted in a reaction by staff that was
ridiculously out of proportion to the crime
commited. If relations and understanding
between staff could be improved in the school it
would, without a doubt, lead to a more
efficient, enjoyable and easier to work system.
Until this is obtained anarchy will rule, future
generations will suffer and school will remain in
the eyes of children a place of hatred, defiance
and above all sheer frustration.
   Boy, Highers. Studying economics at university.

'I THINK YOU SHOULD
TRY MORE TO HELP
US . . . INSTEAD OF
JUST TALKING ALOT
OF RUBBISH ALL THE
TIME TO US. SAYING
YOU'S WILL HELP BUT
YOU'S DONT.
AND I THINK YOU'S
HAVE GOT A CHEEK
ASKING ME TO FILL
THIS IN AFTER ALL
YOU'S SHOULD HAVE
CAME AND TOLD US
WHAT TO DO FOR THE
BEST INSTEAD OFF
ASKING KIDS LOTS OF
THINGS TO HELP
OTHER PEOPLE'

School leaver

Appendix

With the exception of the official figures included as part of Table 1, the tables that follow are based on the weighted returns to the 40 per cent sample survey conducted in 1977 of pupils who had left school in the 1975/6 session. Leavers from education authority and grant-aided schools are included. Leavers from independent schools are excluded. At the non-certificate level the 1977 survey was restricted to leavers in the regions of Fife, Lothian, Strathclyde and Tayside and the Shetland Authority. Together these areas contained about three-quarters of all Scottish leavers in that year. Among those who attempted Highers or only O grades, leavers in all Regions were surveyed. Tables 1–7 are confined to leavers from the mainland authorities for which 1977 information was available at all three levels of school achievement; that is, Fife, Lothian, Strathclyde and Tayside. Information from the 1979 survey is included only in Table 8. At the time of writing the 1979 survey has not been analysed as fully as that of 1977, nor have its data yet been weighted in order to correct for certain sampling and response biases. However, in view of the fact that the majority of the comments are taken from the 1979 survey, we thought it as well to show in Table 8 both the 1977 and the (provisional and unweighted) 1979 figures on the patterning of open-ended comments.

The crosstabulations in Tables 1–7 give the reader a framework within which to locate our selection of accounts and the content of those accounts. Tables 1–6 are about leavers and, broadly, show the extent to which the experience of belting, truancy and unemployment was concentrated among non-certificate pupils and leavers. Those who enjoyed their final school year, or who found it worthwhile, tended to be the certificate pupils and especially those who went on to Highers. Table 7 is about schools rather than about pupils; that is, it shows the extent to which the experiences of pupils described by Tables 2–6 tended to be concentrated in just a small proportion of schools, or, alternatively, spread more evenly over all schools.

The areas of the figures that accompany the tables are approximate. In particular slight differences between the sexes in the percentages of O grade and non-certificate leavers are not shown.

Apart from the official figures in Table 1, and the information in Table 7 that was derived from a data-set in which pupils' experiences were 'aggregated-up', school by school, all of the information in the tables is publicly available for re-analysis. Indeed through the SSRC's programme of 'Collaborative Research' at the Edinburgh University Centre for Educational Sociology, a great variety of information on different topics can now be used in local settings by educational practitioners and others. The information extends from the early sixties to the survey of 1979 and will eventually include the 1981 survey, currently in its planning stage. More information on how one may participate in this programme of research is given after the tables.

Table 1: Comparison between official population percentages of leavers with different qualifications and the 1977 sample survey's estimates of the same.

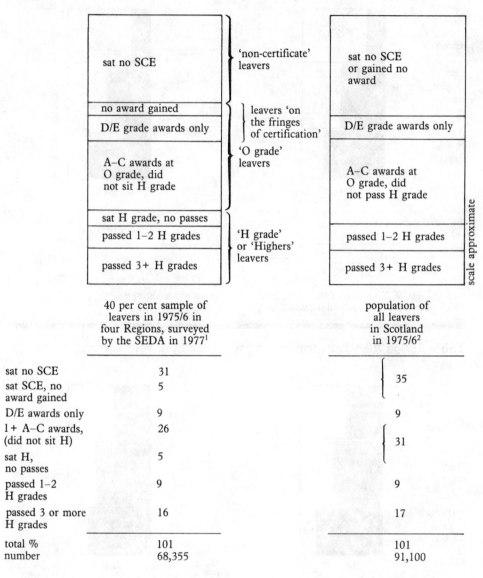

	40 per cent sample of leavers in 1975/6 in four Regions, surveyed by the SEDA in 1977[1]	population of all leavers in Scotland in 1975/6[2]
sat no SCE	31	35
sat SCE, no award gained	5	
D/E awards only	9	9
1+ A–C awards, (did not sit H)	26	31
sat H, no passes	5	
passed 1–2 H grades	9	9
passed 3 or more H grades	16	17
total %	101	101
number	68,355	91,100

[1] The 1977 sample survey is more fully described in Raffe, Lamb *et al.*, 1978. The four Regions for which full data were available in the 1977 survey were Strathclyde, Lothian, Fife and Tayside. They accounted for roughly three-quarters of the Scottish school population. The values given here are weighted estimates based on an unweighted sample of approximately 16,000 cases. For details of weighting see *idem.*, Appendix E. Grant-aided schools are included but independent schools are excluded.

[2] Source: SED *Assessment for All*. Edinburgh. HMSO, 1977. Table C1, p.131. The fuller details shown for the sample survey data are not available for the official figures in this source.

Table 2: 'On the whole, do you feel that your last year at school was worthwhile? yes/no'*

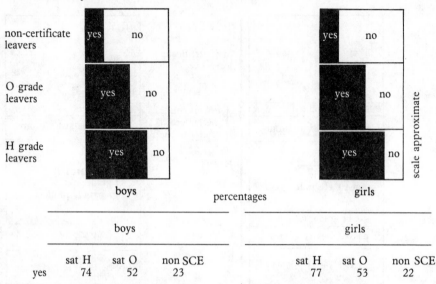

	boys				girls		
	sat H	sat O	non SCE		sat H	sat O	non SCE
yes	74	52	23		77	53	22

* In the non-SCE version of the questionnaire the question was shorter:
'Was your last year at school worthwhile?'

Table 3: 'On the whole, would you say you enjoyed your last year at school? yes/no'*

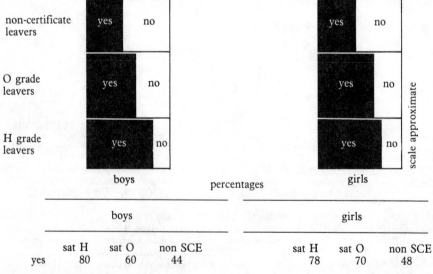

	boys				girls		
	sat H	sat O	non SCE		sat H	sat O	non SCE
yes	80	60	44		78	70	48

* In the non-SCE version of the questionnaire the question was shorter:
'Did you enjoy your last year at school?'

Table 4: 'Did you play truant in your fourth year at school? never/a lesson here and there/a day here and there/several days at a time/weeks at a time'*

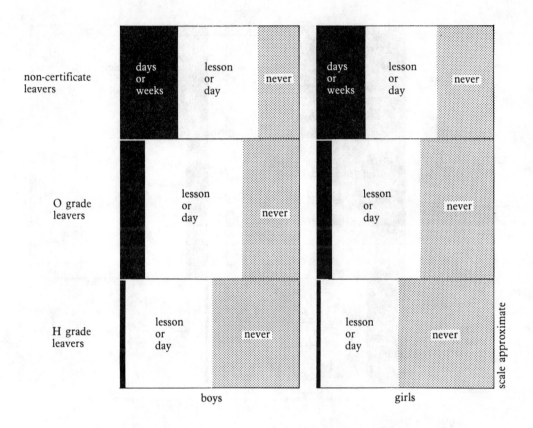

percentages

	boys				girls		
	sat H	sat O	non SCE		sat H	sat O	non SCE
never	47	31	23		52	41	32
lesson here and there	38	25	15		38	26	17
day here and there	14	32	30		11	24	26
several days at a time	1	8	15		1	6	13
weeks at a time	§	4	17		§	3	13
all	100	100	100		102	100	101

* In the non-SCE version of the questionnaire the question was: 'Did you ever play truant in your last year at school?'
§ less than 0.5 per cent.

Table 5: 'Did you ever get the belt, strap or other form of corporal punishment at secondary school? never/once or twice/quite often/often?'*

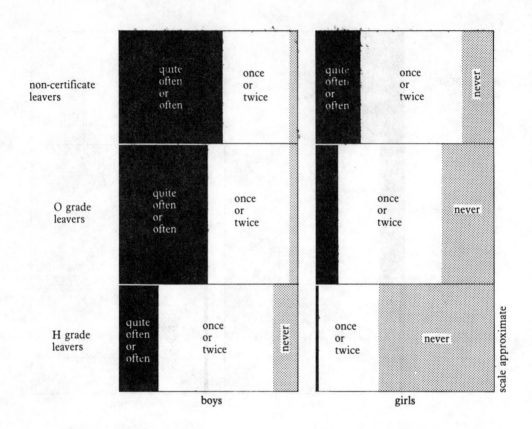

	percentages						
	boys				girls		
	sat H	sat O	non SCE		sat H	sat O	non SCE
never	12	3	3		64	28	18
once or twice	66	47	37		35	58	57
quite often	18	33	33		2	10	16
often	5	17	27		§	4	10
all	101	100	100		101	100	101

* In the non-SCE version of the questionnaire the question was shorter: 'Did you ever get the belt or strap at secondary school?'
§ less than 0.5 per cent.

Table 6: Destination (as at January after leaving school)

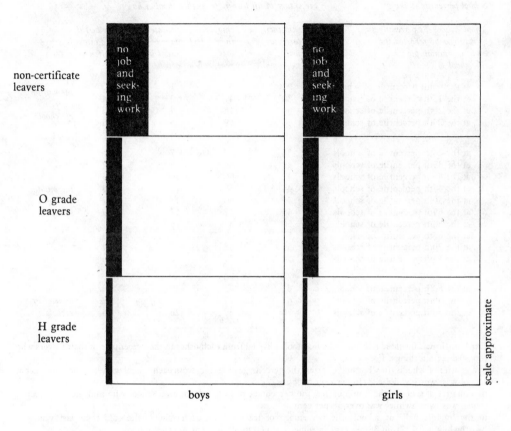

boys   girls

scale approximate

percentages

	boys				girls		
	sat H	sat O	non SCE		sat H	sat O	non SCE
full-time job	45	87	73		47	75	69
full-time education	46	3	1		47	14	3
unemployed and seeking work	4	8	24		2	8	23
others	6	2	3		4	3	5
all	101	100	101		100	100	101

Table 7: The range of difference between schools in the percentage of their leavers who reported various events or opinions.

School percentile ranking   *percentage of all leavers from the schools who . . .*

schools where the percentages of leavers who reported the event or opinion placed the school	*. . . said their last year was worthwhile*	*. . . enjoyed their last year*	*. . . truanted days or weeks at a time*	*. . . were belted quite often or often*	
. . . at the tenth percentile of schools	27	37	1	0	*the bottom*
. . . at the 15th percentile of schools	32	41	3	4	*quarter*
. . . at the 20th percentile of schools	34	45	4	7	*of schools*
. . . at the 25th percentile of schools	36	49	6	8	
. . . at the 30th percentile of schools	38	52	7	10	
. . . at the 35th percentile of schools	40	54	8	12	
. . . at the 40th percentile of schools	42	56	10	13	
. . . at the 45th percentile of schools	44	58	11	15	*the middle*
. . . at the 50th percentile of schools	46	60	13	17	*half of*
. . . at the 55th percentile of schools	48	62	14	19	*schools*
. . . at the 60th percentile of schools	50	63	15	21	
. . . at the 65th percentile of schools	53	66	17	23	
. . . at the 70th percentile of schools	55	68	18	24	
. . . at the 75th percentile of schools	58	71	20	26	
. . . at the 80th percentile of schools	62	73	22	28	*the top*
. . . at the 85th percentile of schools	67	77	24	32	*quarter of*
. . . at the 90th percentile of schools	70	80	26	36	*schools*

Explanation: This table tells how much schools differed from each other in the percentage of their leavers who reported certain things. For example:

in a quarter of schools (the 'bottom' quarter) the percentage of leavers from each school who said their last year at school was 'worthwhile' was 36 per cent or less

in a quarter of schools (the 'top' quarter) the percentage of leavers from each school who said their last year at school was 'worthwhile' was over 58 per cent

in the 'middle half' of schools the percentage of leavers from each school who said their last year was 'worthwhile' varied from 38 per cent in some school(s) to 58 per cent in other school(s).

The same logic may be applied to the columns describing variation between schools in respect of enjoyment, truanting and belting.

Notes: Based on 296 schools.

For the precise question and response wording see Tables 2–5

Leaver percentages have been interpolated where necessary

The position of individual schools in the percentile rank ordering may vary from one column to the next

Table 8: Percentage of leavers that volunteered open-ended comments cross-tabulated by a selection of their opinions about school, their experience of belting and truancy, their post-school destination, and by sex, level of SCE presentation, and the year of the survey.

		no SCE presentation/award*				sat O (but not H) grade				sat H grade			
		boys		girls		boys		girls		boys		girls	
		77	79	77	79	77	79	77	79	77	79	77	79
last year worthwhile?	yes	48	53	70	70	24	36	29	49	36	51	35	50
	no	51	50	64	66	29	36	33	50	38	40	35	51
enjoyed last year?	yes	45	54	66	66	24	33	27	47	35	49	31	50
	no	48	53	64	62	30	38	38	55	39	49	45	53
truanted in fourth year?	never	42	51	62	64	24	29	28	49	34	47	35	49
	lesson	49	49	64	67	25	41	30	49	37	49	34	51
	day	47	50	60	67	30	39	31	47	41	51	39	53
	days	45	54	67	71	31	(43)	48	(60)	58	(88)	31	(73)
	weeks	52	57	64	73	31	(53)	43	(82)	(29)	(50)	(0)	(—)
belted at secondary school?	never	54	(33)	64	63	19	21	24	43	33	50	33	50
	once or twice	51	50	68	69	27	36	31	53	34	48	37	49
	quite often	45	48	65	74	27	33	33	(51)	39	54	20	(73)
	often	51	53	80	69	26	33	48	(40)	44	44	(100)	(71)
destination†	f.t. job	45	50	61	66	26	36	30	50	33	45	34	50
	f.t. education	50	(62)	60	69	22	(32)	31	46	39	53	37	52
	unemployed	51	56	70	72	34	(36)	33	48	43	(45)	27	(65)
	all	46	51	63	67	25	36	29	49	36	49	35	50

Explanation: The table shows the percentages of different types of respondent that volunteered comments. It thereby allows one to judge how far the comments as a whole came from a representative group of leavers. The most relevant comparison to make is between adjacent column percentages. For example the top left hand value tells us that among non-certificate boys in 1977 who said their last year had been 'worthwhile', 48 per cent commented; among their counterparts, immediately below, who said their last year had not been 'worthwhile', virtually the same proportion, 51 per cent commented; and so on.
Notes: * The 1977 figures in the columns headed 'no presentation/award' are based on leavers who had sat no SCE examinations; the 1979 figures also include leavers who received only D and E grades in the O grade examinations. D and E are commonly regarded as 'fail' grades.
The 1979 figures for all leavers are provisional pending the weighting of the 1979 data. The 1977 figures are weighted (see Raffe, Lamb *et al.* 1978, Appendix E).
Some questions were asked only of sub-samples.
The wording of the questions and the answer categories is given in full in Tables 2 to 5.
( ) indicates that the value is a percentage of a base of less than 50 weighted cases.
The precise wording of the questions that prompted the comments is given in the Introduction.
The prompts for O and H grade leavers in 1977 were very brief.
† f.t.: full-time.

The Collaborative Research Programme
(adapted from Collaborative Research Newsletter 7, June 1980)

What is collaborative research? It is a programme based on the Centre for Educational Sociology at Edinburgh University which gives people the opportunity to carry out research into Scottish education and to follow up questions that interest them about school leavers. Funding is from the Social Science Research Council. The Centre also receives financial and other support from the SED and other bodies.

What information is available? The Scottish Education Data Archive (SEDA) is a computerised data bank of information on Scottish school leavers containing information relating to pupils who left school in 1962/3, 1969/70, 1971/2, 1975/6 and 1978/9. Recent questionnaires covered such issues as curricular choices, examination results, attitudes to personal and careers guidance, choice of higher education institutions, the experience of work or of unemployment, and a variety of other topics. The answers can be used to illuminate both local and national situations. A survey of 1979/80 leavers is also to be placed in the SEDA in 1982.

How is collaborative research done? Both by individuals and working parties. Access to publicly available data is free and unrestricted. It is not necessary to have any previous knowledge of research techniques, statistics or computers. Courses and advice are provided. The principles of respondent and school anonymity are observed.

Who can participate in the research? Any individual or body interested in Scottish education. There are various working parties, some more formally constituted than others. For instance, there is a working party of Regional Education Authority officials and one of representatives of the ten Colleges of Education. Other groups, such as teachers or careers officers, meet on a more *ad hoc* basis for brief sessions or for more sustained work over longer periods of time.

Funding for the current phase of the Collaborative Research Programme will terminate in 1982.

Summary details of the topics covered in the 1977 and 1979 National School Leavers Surveys

(*adapted from Collaborative Research Newsletter 6, December 1979*)

(an asterisk indicates that information is available)

	H Grade	O Grade	Non-certificate
age	★	★	★
sex	★	★	★
school type	★	★	★
school denomination	★	★	★
school region & area	★	★	★
parental education & occupation	★	★	★
travelling, hostel residence	★	★	
results in school examinations	★	★	
subjects taken/dropped	★	★	★
non-examinable subjects	★	★	★
reason for taking/not taking subjects	★	★	
work experience	★	★	★
link courses	★	★	★
attitudes to school experience	★	★	★
truancy	★	★	★
corporal punishment	★	★	★
study methods/school pedagogy	★	★	
attitudes to exams	★	★	★
attitudes to curriculum	★	★	★
reasons for leaving/staying	★	★	
experience of & attitudes to sixth year	★		
curricular & vocational guidance received	★	★	★
school clubs, community facilities	★	★	
post-school destination	★	★	★
tertiary education course	★	★	★
employment/unemployment	★	★	★
applications, information & choices	★	★	
occupational intentions, expected income	★	★	
job selection	★	★	★
occupational training & satisfaction	★	★	★
travel to work		★	★
difficulty in getting job			★
Youth Opportunities Programmes	★	★	★

Full information is available in Raffe, Lamb *et al.* (1978).

References

* **Ballantyne, W. and Taylor, D. (1979)** 'They may not love us more, but they hate us less: The CSE experience'. *Collaborative Research Newsletter*, 6, December. CES Edinburgh.
Using the SEDA and other sources, two teachers from Garnock Academy show the extent to which the SCE O grade exam is too difficult for most pupils who do not take Highers. They also review their experience of using CSE Mode III courses as an alternative or supplement.

* **Bibby, J. and Weston, P. B. (1980)** 'Sex Differentials in Maths Enrolments: sudden death or gradual decline'. *Collaborative Research Newsletter*, 7, June. CES Edinburgh.
Contains figures on the wastage from Mathematics courses leading to SCE O grade presentation.

Blishen, E. (Ed.) (1973) *The School That I'd Like:* Penguin Education Special. Harmondsworth.
In these extracts from entries to an essay competition organised by *The Observer* newspaper on the topic 'The School That I'd Like', the writers, mostly secondary school children, describe shortcomings in existing educational provision and what might improve matters.

* **Centre for Educational Sociology (1979)** 'A Code of Practice for Collaborative Research'. *Collaborative Research Newsletter*, 6, December. CES Edinburgh.
A code of practice to be observed by those wishing to analyse data in the SEDA.

* **Cope, E. and Gray, J. (1978)** 'Figures and perspectives on the national problem of truancy: an opening discussion'. *Collaborative Research Newsletter*, 3, June. CES Edinburgh.
Describes the distribution over Scotland of self-reported truancy in S4, discusses the validity and reliability of the measures and describes a content-analysis of pupils' reasons for playing truant.

* **Cosford, B. (1978)** 'Imagine the school asking me!' *Collaborative Research Newsletter*, 3, June. CES Edinburgh.
An interview study of 25 recipients of the 1977 non-certificate questionnaire that tried to throw light on how leavers had understood and reacted to it.

* **Dickson, C. (1979)** 'The state of modern languages'. *Collaborative Research Newsletter*, 5, June. CES Edinburgh.
Contains figures on, and a discussion of, wastage from language courses leading to presentation at the SCE O grade.

* **Freeman, J. and Staite, R. (1978)** 'Basic skills and pupil motivation'. *Collaborative Research Newsletter*, 3, June. CES Edinburgh.
Discusses the implications of non-certificate leavers self-assessed competence in literacy and numeracy and their need for more help with these basic skills.

* Material about the SEDA, or using data from it, is indicated with an asterisk.

* **Gray, J. and McPherson, A. F. (1979)** *Figuring It Out: a course of self-instruction on the Scottish Education Data Archive.* CES Edinburgh.
Together with the 'Dictionary' and questionnaires (Raffe, Lamb *et al.* (1978)), this introductory course enables the remote user to write simple requests for information from the SEDA. Attendance at the two-day introductory courses is also advised.

* **A Group of Principal Careers Officers (1978)** 'Unemployed school leavers: The Holland challenge to education and the careers service'. *Collaborative Research Newsletter,* 3, June. CES Edinburgh.
Discusses the problems of unemployment facing non-certificate leavers and their likely response to the provisions of the Youth Opportunities Programme in the light of their reactions to link courses, to work experience schemes and to part-time jobs held while at school.

* **McPherson, A. F. and Raffe, D. (1978)** 'Some political and social influences on a national education survey'. Paper read by A. F. McPherson to the Edinburgh local group of the Royal Statistical Society, Edinburgh, November 1978.
Describes the development of the biennial school leavers' survey conducted by the CES at the University of Edinburgh and gives details of losses occuring at the sampling and response stages which give an optimistic bias to some conclusions.

* **McPherson, A. F., Raab, C. D. and Raffe, D. (1978)** 'Social explanation and political accountability: two related problems with a single solution'. Paper presented to the Annual Conference of the British Educational Research Association, Leeds, September.
Describes the practice and philosophy of a programme of 'collaborative' research based on the CES at the University of Edinburgh, which aims to involve researchers and practitioners alike in the use of research methods to understand educational issues.

* **Raffe, D. (1980a)** 'School Leavers' Jobs and FE'. *Collaborative Research Newsletter,* 7, June. CES Edinburgh.
Describes the present association between levels of certification and types of employment among Scottish school leavers.

* **Raffe, D. (1980b)** 'Special Programmes in Scotland in the first year of YOP'. *CES working paper.* Edinburgh.
Evaluates the Youth Opportunities Programme in Scotland.

* **Raffe, D. (1980c)** 'Link courses in Scotland'. *Educational Research,* 22, 2, February.
Evaluates the introduction into Scottish schools of courses linking schools with FE colleges.

* **Raffe, D. and Lamb, J. et al. (1978)** *Collaborative Research Dictionary 1977* and *Collaborative Research Questionnaires 1977.* CES Edinburgh.
Contain full details of the conduct and documentation of the 1977 survey.

School of Barbiana (1970) *Letter to a Teacher.* Penguin Education Special. Harmondsworth.
Helped by their priest and teacher, boys from the school at Barbiana responded to failures in the State's provision by developing their own critique of education.

Scottish Education Department, Advisory Council on Education in Scotland (1947) *Secondary Education.* HMSO Edinburgh. Cmnd. 7005.
The finest statement of the Scottish humanist tradition in education.

Scottish Education Department (1966) Education in Scotland in 1965. HMSO Edinburgh. Cmnd. 2914.
Contains details of the types of secondary schools in Scotland in 1965.

Scottish Education Department, Liaison Committee on Educational Matters (1968) *Statement of Principles and Code of Practice.* HMSO Edinburgh.
Principles and practice recommended to local education authorities regarding the use of corporal punishment in Scottish schools.

Scottish Education Department (1976) *Report on the Raising of the School Leaving Age in Scotland.* HMSO Edinburgh.
Describes official provision for ROSLA and identifies failures to develop or implement adequate curricula for non-certificate pupils.

Scottish Education Department. Committee of Inquiry into Truancy and Indiscipline in Schools in Scotland (1977) *Report.* HMSO Edinburgh. ('The Pack Report')
The main source of information and advice on truancy and indiscipline in Scottish schools in the mid seventies.

Scottish Education Department. Committee on the Structure of the Curriculum in the Third and Fourth Years of the Scottish Secondary School (1977) *Report.* HMSO Edinburgh. ('The Munn Report')
Recommended a 'core plus options' curriculum for all pupils in their last two years of compulsory schooling.

Scottish Education Department. Committee to Review Assessment in the Third and Fourth Years of Secondary Education in Scotland (1979). *Assessment for All.* HMSO Edinburgh. ('The Dunning Report')
Recommended a three tier national examination at 16 years for virtually all pupils, containing elements of both internal and external assessment.

Scottish Education Department (1980) *The Munn and Dunning Reports: The Government's Development Programme.* HMSO Edinburgh.
A resumé of recent proposals for changes in curriculum and assessment in the final years of compulsory education and a new proposal to leave unchanged the externally set and assessed SCE H and O grade examinations while introducing a new examination, mainly for the current type of non-certificate pupil, containing both external and internal elements.